Anthony Holt MBE was a pilot and seaman officer in the Royal Navy for 30 years, leaving as a Commander in 1992 to run the Naval and Military Club in Piccadilly, and then the Army and Navy Club in Pall Mall.

His naval service took him around the world including a two year spell on loan to the Australian Navy, spent first as Senior Pilot of the helicopter training squadron then at sea in the aircraft carrier *Melbourne*.

He is married and lives in Dorset, where he spends his time writing, sailing, working as a Volunteer Coast Watcher and as a member of the local Harbour Board, in addition to entertaining his four grandchildren.

At Least We Didn't Sink!

(The Adventures of a Pommie Pilot in the last Australian
Aircraft Carrier)

Also by the Same Author

Spoofy, (Vanguard Press), 2012
ISBN: 978 1 84386 886 6

Anthony Holt

At Least We Didn't Sink!

Vanguard Press

VANGUARD PAPERBACK

© Copyright 2013
Anthony Holt

A CIP catalogue record for this title is
available from the British Library.

ISBN 978 1 84386 793 0

*Vanguard Press is an imprint of
Pegasus Elliot MacKenzie Publishers Ltd.*
www.pegasuspublishers.com

First Published in 2013

**Vanguard Press
Sheraton House Castle Park
Cambridge England**

Printed and bound in Great Britain

*To the late Commander Jim Firth RAN, a never failing,
resourceful and irrepressible friend.*

Acknowledgements

This is the story centred on my own experiences, ashore and afloat. It could not be complete without the input of others and in several instances I have used anecdotes told to me by British and Australian friends.

Again, I must acknowledge the unstinting help and support of my wife, Irene, always ready to solve problems of memory and production.

Glossary of Terms

Accommodation Ladder

A stairway which is hung from the ship's side enabling people to climb to the deck from a boat at the waterline.

Big Black Welcoming Dog

See my book *Spoofy*

Brow

Another term for the gangway — the wooden or metal footbridge connecting the ship to shore when in harbour.

Cabin Flat

An area which is only part of a deck, forming a space giving access to cabins.

CAG Commander

The officer in command of the Carrier Air Group which includes all embarked squadrons.

Catapult Launch

The take-off of a fixed-wing aircraft assisted by being attached to a wire running along a track in the flight deck. Using the power of steam the catapult is thrust rapidly forward, flinging the aircraft into the air, whence

	its own power will keep it flying.
Changi, Seletar, Nee Soon	Small villages in Singapore outside the city.
Chief of Staff	The officer who heads and controls an admirals staff. Second in command to the admiral
Chiefs' Mess	The communal Chief Petty Officers' "lounge" where they socialise but do not necessarily sleep.
Clips on Watertight Doors	Big steel bars which are connected through the adjacent structure on each side of a watertight steel door, and when moved by turning they will press the door tightly into its frame, making it watertight.
Divisions	A major parade of officers and ratings in a Naval ship or establishment.
Echelon	Aircraft flying in a diagonal line from the leader – rather in the style of geese.

Flying Stations	A state of readiness for the launch and landing of aircraft.
Gangway	A portable footbridge connecting the ship to the jetty. Also refers to the area around the entry point to the ship from where the ship's routine is controlled in harbour.
Green Clad	Refers to aircrew flying suits which are jungle green in colour.
Harbour Stations	The deployment of crewmen for entering or leaving harbour.
Heads	Lavatories.
Indian Style Crawl	Creeping forward while remaining flat on the floor.
Kai Tais	Young male transvestites peculiar to Singapore who dress in a spectacularly glamorous style and who spend their evenings at the red light district. By day they often work as smart young men in the commercial district.

Libertymen	Ratings (sailors) allowed ashore on leave.
Mae West	A specialised lifejacket used by aircrew, including a two way radio and homing beacon, mini-flares, shark repellent, heliograph etc.
Mess	A space where sailors live, communally, forming a small community.
Mirror Officer	The officer (usually a pilot) in charge of the aircraft carriers mirror deck landing system, an aid to pilots of fixed-wing aircraft attempting to land on the deck.
Master at Arms	The senior non-commissioned officer in a ship. Additionally he is the ship's "Chief of Police". A powerful individual.
Observer	An aircrew officer whose duties encompass navigation and tactical control.
Planeguard	A ship or helicopter nominated to wait alongside the aircraft carrier while it is

operating aircraft, in order to recover survivors from crashed aircraft.

Round Down.

The curved deck surface at the stern of a flight deck allowing greater safety in the event of a short landing.

Snowdrop

A United States Navy policeman, so named for the white helmet they wear.

Station Cards

A small card given to each person onboard recording name, watch, emergency station etc. It must be handed in when a sailor goes ashore and collected on return so that the number and names of personnel ashore are recorded.

Task Force

A military grouping of warships, support ships and aircraft under a single designated command.

Chapter 1

Hello *Melbourne*

"My God! Does *that* actually go to sea?"

We stood in the warm autumn sunshine looking down from the Sydney Botanical Gardens towards Garden Island Dockyard which was dominated by the grey and rust-coloured shape of Her Majesty's Australian Ship *Melbourne*. We had spent the last twelve hours or so sleeping in our high-rise hotel room, trying to shift the clinging jet lag and intermittently waking to deal with the essential needs of our five-week-old baby, but had finally ventured out into the bright spring day to take in our first impressions of the exciting experience of a new land far from home.

It was early April when forty-eight hours previously we had left a cold, wet and blustery Heathrow Airport to fly halfway round the world. A day and a half later we had stepped out into clear skies, warm sunshine and balmy breezes. After the night in our Phillip Street hotel room we all needed the rejuvenating effect of some fresh air. Once the baby was organised and fed we set out to take in the sights and sounds of Australia. Having reassembled the baby's lightweight pram we began to walk the short distance to the Botanical Gardens. The day was idyllic. Warm with just enough breeze to ruffle the leaves and with a brightness and crispness in the daylight that really lifted the heart.

We had strolled around the gardens for a while taking in the plants and bird life, much of which was new to us, and now we were standing on the high ground overlooking the naval base and dockyard situated below us on Garden Island. Away to our right was the bright blue expanse of the harbour with a small island in the foreground. Further round, the skyline was dominated by the famous harbour bridge, known as the 'coat hanger' to some of the locals. Over to our left the sunshine sparkled and glittered off the high rise buildings of the great city stretching away to the south.

The shocked remark had been uttered by my wife, Irene, when I had pointed out to her the flagship and sole remaining aircraft carrier of the Royal Australian Navy. I was a naval pilot and now we were all taking in the Australian sunshine by order of the Admiralty Board who had decreed that for the next two years I should apply my skills to the benefit of Australia – specifically to their Navy. Somewhere in our luggage I had the single sheet of paper appointing me to *HMAS Albatross*, the base of the Australian Fleet Air Arm a hundred miles to the south, so I knew that there was minimal risk of any close association in the immediate future with the tired-looking ship lying in front of us.

We sat on the grass, while our little daughter continued to doze in comfort, and we both resumed our critical study of the mighty warship. Irene frowned as she took in the dishevelled state of the vessel and although I was more familiar with ships in dockyard hands I could not see much to commend this one to me. She really did look a sad mess, more fit for the breaker's yard than for any future seagoing career, I thought. All the grey paint looked dirty and dull and there were extensive areas of rust covering the ship's side and parts of the superstructure. Three cranes were bent over the after part of the flight deck but none of them seemed to be doing anything. The rest of the flight deck had almost disappeared under a network of hoses, pipes and thick black electric cables.

Such space as was left had been filled up with boxes, bits of machinery, tractors and other vehicles. At least four scruffy and unadorned gangways sloped up from the dockside, these being strung with even more pipes, hoses and cables. I noticed that the ship flew no ensign so she was not in commission.

I allowed my gaze to wander over the rest of the dockyard. There was very little activity but, being Sunday, this was unsurprising. Many of the other berths were taken up with efficient and sharp-looking destroyers and frigates with a clutch of smaller patrol boats and minesweepers, two submarines and a solitary tanker. I was looking at most of the small but impressive Australian Navy but the contrast between the clean-cut and professional escorts and the dirty, scruffy aircraft carrier only seemed to make the big ship look more forlorn and unfit for sea service.

I noticed several figures clad in baggy ill-fitting brown overalls lounging, smoking and drinking tea on the flight deck in front of the island superstructure and I reflected for a moment on 'dockyard mateys'. Here we were on the other side of the world and there they were, dressed the same, acting the same and doing the same minimal work that I had seen so many times in dockyards at home. 'Perhaps there is an international brotherhood' was my unspoken thought as we walked away from our temporary viewing base.

As we strolled back towards our stark and unlovely hotel I reminded Irene that I had been appointed to number 725 Squadron which was shore-based at Nowra, headquarters of the Australian Fleet Air Arm and it was unlikely that I would go to sea in the aircraft carrier, assuming, that is, that it ever went to sea again.

That evening we prepared ourselves for an early start, failed in an attempt to organise a taxi for the next morning, and went to bed hoping to slough off a little more of the effects of our long journey.

Next morning, we found a very large taxi, explained yet again to the receptionist that our bill had already been paid by the Australian Navy, set off for a later train than we had intended and embarked on the last hundred miles to our destination.

****

Fifteen months later I was once again staring down at *HMAS Melbourne*, still moored alongside at Garden Island. This time I was leading a formation of four Wessex Mk 31B anti-submarine helicopters, the second section of number 817 Squadron and we were orbiting Sydney Harbour at one thousand feet waiting for approval to land on the carrier.

"Blue Section, you are cleared to land in turn. Approach from the north-east and look out for high structures to your left on the approach." The clear voice of the controller interrupted my thought process, turning me back to the job in hand.

"Roger Mike Bravo," I responded. "Blue Section, Echelon Port, Echelon Port – Go!"

"Mike Bravo this is Blue Leader. Blue Section descending to five hundred feet. Are we clear for one run past at that height before breaking to land, over?"

"Wait," came the answer.

"Roger, Blue Section copy?"

"Blue two copied."

"Blue three copied."

"Blue four copied."

My boys were with me and understood my intentions. I was reassured.

"Blue Leader, this is Mike Bravo. You are cleared to descend not below five hundred feet for one run – one run only – before breaking to land. Acknowledge."

I had my clearance to do a bit of showing off although it was the most grudging clearance I could imagine. "Descending, running in, tighten up," I spoke calmly into the radio. There was no need for a reply – I looked to my left and my co-pilot raised a thumb, signifying that all was going according to plan and the section was in a nice tight echelon lined away and up to my left. I concentrated on accurate flying, levelling at exactly five hundred feet and ninety knots but I could still see the ship below. I counted the seconds as we passed down her side then called into the radio "Blue Section – Breaking, breaking – Go!" On the word go I pulled into a sharp climbing turn through 180 degrees, established a descent in the downwind position and eased off the speed before turning for the final approach. I could see the four landing spots with a 'batman' in front of each one waiting to wave each aircraft down from the hover.

Five minutes later, we were all down, rotors and engines stopped with aircrew heading for the 'island' while the aircraft handlers got on with the task of folding the rotor blades and tails before wheeling each aircraft to the lift for transport to the hangar. I signed my aircraft in, picked up a sheaf of papers including an important note announcing which cabin I had been allocated and clattered down several ladders to the hangar deck to meet up with my aircraft and recover my kit.

I watched and listened as the bells jangled, warning of the descending lift. As it dropped steadily into the hangar, an expanding square of brilliant blue sky opened above it, lighting up the hangar below and illuminating the blue and white helicopter, now neatly folded, sitting on the lift, waiting to be stowed. A team of aircraft handlers moved smoothly forward as the lift came to a stop level with the hangar deck. One man hopped nimbly up into the cockpit to control the wheel brakes, two more men grasped the towing arm attached to the tail wheel and the fourth, whistle in mouth, moved back into the hangar to direct the manoeuvre. The handlers on the towing arm heaved and several tons of aircraft moved, tail first, surprisingly smoothly off the lift. As soon as it was clear, an arm was raised and the lift started back towards the flight deck, shutting out the daylight and filling the hangar with discordant bell clanging.

I waited until the helicopter was safely stowed and chocked before collecting my kit. I dragged several bags, some cases and one huge aircrew flying clothing holdall out of the aircraft cabin, slid the door shut and established a dump to one side of the heavy watertight steel door leading out of the hangar. As I opened the door to start the combined process of locating my cabin and ferrying my worldly goods and possessions to my new home a familiar figure faced me, in the process of coming through the doorway from the other side. I had learned the proper form of Ozzie greeting and after a short pause I said, "G'day Jim."

The pause was occasioned because it had taken me a moment or two to recognise my old friend, mostly since I was only able to see the upper part of his face. The lower half had disappeared behind a luxuriant, black, frizzy beard. Jim had been an observer with me when I had been Senior Pilot in 725 Squadron but our acquaintance stretched further back than that to when he had arrived on exchange duty at the Naval Air Station in Portland, Dorset several years before.

I had not previously encountered Jim with a beard and I was not sure that the present growth improved his appearance. He immediately began to help lift my baggage through the door and we chatted as we worked.

"What's it like being away from all the action as Squadron Ops, Jim?" I said.

"I'm not away from it, I'm in the thick of it," he countered.

"Not much flying though?"

"Yeah, but that's Sydney out there."

"Good run ashore eh?"

"The best. Not the cheapest though."

"What's with the fuzz?" I asked, changing the subject and looking pointedly at the beard.

"Save all that time shaving," he replied, "and being away, there's no missus around to complain about it." That didn't seem to need an answer and after a pause he continued, "Boss don't like it though."

"Oh yes?" I said.

"Yeah, he said it was like a rat peering out of a bear's arse."

"Hard to counter that one, Jim," I said.

"Yeah, it's a bummer."

All of my kit was now in the corridor, blocking half of it so we set off in the direction of my cabin, Jim leading the way. We went down a ladder and reversed direction, heading aft. A turning off the main passageway led to three cabins. Jim pushed open the door of the one on our left and dropped my bags inside. I did the same and glanced around at the cabin interior. I was pleased with what I saw. For a warship cabin there was a lot of space and it looked as though it may at one time have provided accommodation for two or even three officers. It had the usual bunk perched on top of a fitted metal unit housing tiers of drawers and a desk with a fold-down front. Above the bunk was a shelf and over in the far corner a washbasin. Around to my right were the metal double doors of a modestly sized wardrobe, with a row of coat hooks beyond, all leaving plenty of space for my folding armchair and my other bits and pieces.

As I stepped out into the corridor Jim said, "I'm just across here," as he proudly threw open the door of the cabin opposite. I looked in, to a cabin of similar size to mine but in a state of chaotic terminal decline.

"When did the bomb go off?" I asked quietly.

Jim gave me an old-fashioned look and said, "Easy to sort it out. It'll be 'Bristol' before we run ashore." I began to backtrack. I wasn't ready for one of Jim's famously uninhibited runs ashore, and anyway, my wife and child were about to arrive in a nearby hotel, probably, I thought, expecting me to join them!

"Later, Jim," I said. "At least wait 'til we deploy." With a shrug, he accepted this and wandered off to do 'Ops-like' things, while I retraced my steps to collect the last of my belongings. I called after him, "Thanks Jim."

He waved a hand as he walked away.

"No worries!"

****

For eighteen months I had been enjoying the life of a sailor home from the sea, albeit in a temporary home on the other side of the world. I had been able to settle into family life, enjoying the simple steady routine contrasting with a climate of almost permanent summer, or so it seemed in comparison with the unpredictable and sometimes downright hostile weather at our real home in Dorset.

It had, for me, been a sombre morning made even more so by the false cheerfulness which seemed to surround me. My wife was already used to the pressures and sadness all naval wives have to cope with when their husbands are routinely called away to duty on the oceans of the world but my little daughter had yet to experience life without Daddy. The other member of my family behaved as if he knew exactly what was about to happen. Spoofy was a big black Labrador who had attached himself to my family almost as soon as we had set up home in Nowra and only shortly before his real owners were to depart for a two-year spell in England. He had seemed to know then that he needed to take action to secure himself a new home, and now that same ability to 'know' was keeping him close to home and close to me during my preparations for departure.

As my wife, Irene, drove me away in the car, with our daughter Rebecca, cooing from her strapped-in position in the back seat, I could see Spoofy sitting bolt upright in the entrance to our driveway, staring with his liquid brown eyes after the car as we disappeared in the direction of the air station. Irene and Rebecca were to go up to Sydney for the last few days before the big ship sailed and I would see them before we left. But I would not see the big scruffy dog we had all learned to love and as far as he was concerned it might well have been a parting forever.

****

I was halfway through stowing my kit when there was a tap on the door and the fresh face of a young midshipman peered into the cabin.

"Squadron meeting sir, ten minutes sir," he said, disappearing before I had time to ask him where the meeting was to take place. I thought for a moment or two and concluded that the meeting would be either in one of the two briefing rooms or in the wardroom. I had not yet visited either location but I had a broad idea that the briefing rooms would not be far below the hangar deck and the wardroom would be somewhere towards the after end of the ship. I need not have worried. I stepped out of my cabin and into the main corridor to see a stream of familiar faces, all clearly aircrew, clad in lightweight green flying overalls, all heading in the same direction. I joined the stream and in only a few minutes found myself entering 'aircrew country'. There were two briefing rooms, back to back, to be shared by three squadrons. Briefing Room 'A' was allocated to the two fixed-wing squadrons and Briefing Room B was to be the exclusive domain of Number 817 Wessex Helicopter Squadron.

With twenty-four pilots, twelve observers, twelve aircrewmen, three engineers and two Helicopter Control Officers and only thirty-eight seats the room was really crowded. Most of the officers were slumped in the airliner-type seats which were fixed to the floor in rows while the aircrewmen and a few others perched on the chart table running down one side of the room and across the back wall. I parked myself on the end of the second row and waited, lost in the hubbub of conversation, for something to happen. After about ten minutes a couple of Air Traffic Control officers arrived, spread some charts in front of the roller blackboard and droned their way through approach patterns, deck lighting systems, planeguard stations, radio frequencies and a load of other necessary but uninspiring trivia which is the lot of the embarked aviator. The younger of the two officers spent some time explaining the duties of a planeguard helicopter. The nominated planeguard helicopter was to be fully equipped for the rescue of ditched aircrew and was to be stationed in a low hover on the port side of the ship's bow for all take-offs and in a similar position near to the port quarter for all landings.

"Nothing new there, then," said a cynical voice from the back of the room.

"Any questions?" said the presentation leader. There were no questions.

As they gathered their bits and pieces the Squadron Boss moved across to the telephone by the door and made a short call. He turned back into the room and said, "OK cut the noise." Obediently, everyone stopped talking and an expectant hush spread over the room. After a minute or two the doorway was filled with a gleaming white tropical uniform surmounted by a head of elegant silver-grey hair under a beautiful Gieves cap with the 'scrambled egg' of a commander decorating the peak. Everyone clambered respectfully to their feet. This was CAG – the Carrier Air Group Commander, the officer nominally in charge of all three squadrons making up the Air Group. I was aware that he was supposed to be our leader even when we were ashore at Nowra, but he was very rarely seen and I had never actually spoken to him.

I can't really remember much of what he said except that it contained a lot of 'I's'. It was I did this, I did that, I told this one or that one, and so on. I took an instant and unaccountable dislike to this man and although we hardly spoke for the entire duration of the deployment, the feeling did not go away. Looking around, I could see that many of the old hands were trying hard, and failing, not to look bored and I learned later that we 'chopper pukes' would be left largely alone while our white-suited hero concentrated on the rather more glamorous fixed-wing boys.

The lecture ended by reminding us all that *Melbourne* was an old and proud ship, followed by a few statistics and historical notes. I perked up a bit because I didn't really know a lot about the ship – other than that she was the only aircraft carrier known to have rammed and cut in half two other ships in peacetime. Both of these ships had been in the planeguard role.

Melbourne was indeed an old ship. She had been part of the massive British shipbuilding programme in the latter part of the Second World War but being launched in 1945 she was just too late to take part in it. She was commissioned as *HMS Majestic*, the leader of a class of six light fleet carriers, most of which were sold or given away to other navies. In 1947, together with her sister ship *HMS Terrible*, she was transferred to the Royal Australian Navy. She became *HMAS Melbourne* and *HMS Terrible* became *HMAS Sydney*. *Sydney* had since been reconfigured as a store ship used largely in support of the Australian contingent in Vietnam.

In 1949 *Melbourne* had begun an extensive refit, including the fitting of an angled flight deck and a steam catapult. It was not until 1955 that she was re-commissioned into the RAN and became operational, with an Air Group of eight Sea Venom fighters, sixteen ungainly Fairy Gannet anti-submarine aircraft and two Bristol Sycamore helicopters for 'planeguard' duties. On 10th February 1964 she collided with the Australian Daring class destroyer *Voyager* which sank with great loss of life. Three Royal Commissions failed to find out unequivocally who was at fault. Five years later, on 3rd of June 1969, she collided with and sank the American destroyer *Frank E. Evans*. It was generally conceded that on this occasion the responsibility for the collision lay with the "*Evans*" but that didn't seem to have done much for *Melbourne's* reputation.

So although only operational for some sixteen years she was in fact, at twenty-six, a very old ship – and some would say a somewhat unlucky ship. All this was going through my mind as I was making my way back to my cabin to continue unpacking. I wondered, as I strolled along the passageway, whether the newly arrived squadron officers would be introduced to the Captain or the other senior officers. Curiously we never were. We seemed to be tolerated within the wardroom but never properly accepted as part of the ship's company.

****

The next couple of days were very quiet. The ship's company continued their preparations for sea, with a seemingly never ending trail of sailors carrying boxes, packages and other paraphernalia, down into the ship, as they were dumped on the flight deck by the dockside cranes. We assembled in the briefing room at 0800 each morning to receive a met briefing, presumably to keep the met officers in practice, followed by a series of instructions on our activities for the rest of the morning. By lunchtime each day we had run out of things to do so we would disperse to amuse ourselves. For my part, I lost no time in heading off, usually by expensive taxi, to meet Irene and Rebecca in their hotel.

We were issued with numerous bits of paper on which we had to obtain signatures from a selection of worthies, largely, I thought, to prove their – or our – existence. Groups of aircrew were then led off to identify our emergency stations where we were issued with ship's lifejackets, which I thought were a poor exchange for the aircrew Mae West lifejackets we habitually wore when flying. We were paraded outside the sickbay to waste our time while a junior surgeon lieutenant confirmed that everything he wanted to do to us had already been done by his colleagues ashore. Then we were given a ship's tour; divided into small groups and led around by midshipmen or sub-lieutenants to visit the boiler rooms, engine room, operations room, Flyco (the aircraft carrier's equivalent of an aerodrome's control tower) and, holy of holies, the Bridge. In fact *Melbourne* had a 'Flag Bridge' as well as the navigational Bridge. This provided additional space for the Admiral and his staff to work in and direct the fleet without tripping over the Captain and the Officers of the Watch.

An aircraft carrier, even a relatively small 'light fleet' carrier such as *Melbourne* is an incredibly complex mix of interrelated machinery, equipment and people. The ship is really a big rectangular box where the top of the box is the flight deck and the box itself is the hangar. Around this key element are fitted three boiler rooms and engine rooms, stores, offices, workshops and various bits of space where the crew must eat, sleep, clean and entertain themselves. No space is wasted and everywhere is just big enough for the intended purpose – no more. Just over five hundred officers and men were required to run the twenty thousand ton ship but when the air group embarked the ship's company rose to nearly twelve hundred. A lot of give and take was required to make it all work properly.

Every time I found my way back to my cabin and opened the door I had to step over small piles of paper giving guidance or instructions on everything from the wardroom cinema programme to the names of the cabin stewards. Each time I arrived I removed the latest batch and placed them on my desk. However if I left the cabin even for a few minutes I could guarantee that some phantom delivery boy would shove another load of paper under my door.

Because of the sheer bulk and quantity of this former forest I nearly missed a most important slip of paper. This informed me that in two days' time, when the ship was due to leave the dockside and move out to a buoy in the harbour, I was to be given the honour of being Officer of the Day. I fought down an initial urge to panic and resolved to educate myself on all the little peculiarities of the ship's routine. In fact I discovered that I had an Assistant Officer of the Day as well as duty midshipmen and others representing various departments, to whom I could happily delegate almost everything. I also discovered that once we had left the dockside I would move even further back in the scheme of things as the ship would establish sea routine and Officers of the Watch would take charge from the Bridge. Until then I would settle in the wardroom, making occasional forays to the after gangway, allowing the others in my busy little team to buzz around me like worker bees.

Chapter 2

Ernie's Run Ashore

We were due to move away from the dockside during the early afternoon. Before this a 'small' drinks party would be held in the wardroom to mark the move out of dockyard hands and to provide an opportunity to thank the various authorities and individuals who had given that little bit extra to ensure that the ship could reach this point on time and as well prepared as possible. A second parallel party was taking place in the Chief Petty Officers' Mess to thank the charge hands and others who had actually done the work. In the wardroom, the Squadron officers, having little to occupy themselves had pitched into the task of entertaining the guests at the party. In fact as the hour of departure came closer and the various ship's officers slipped away to attend to their duty, the aircrew hosts were left almost alone to meet the difficult challenge of matching drink for drink with their hollow-legged guests.

Although the ship had steam up and was capable of manoeuvring under her own power, she was actually nudged and nosed out into the stream by a team of variously sized dockyard tugs who were choreographed by a scruffy looking pilot enjoying his big moment on the Bridge. The ship's team were also fully closed up on the Bridge, frustrated that they could not yet take control of their mighty charge. On deck, in the side sponsons and on the forecastle and the quarter deck, both of which were situated beneath the flight deck, teams of seamen moved about manning giant wickerwork fenders and handling heaving lines and ropes, all moving seemingly without directions but with evident purpose.

One of the giant anchors had been disconnected from its anchor cable, the bare end of which hung down from the starboard hawse pipe. As the ship was being turned ponderously out into the harbour one of the ship's boats, a small open motorboat, chugged up the starboard side towards a big mooring buoy. As it nosed alongside the buoy, two lithe young sailors detached themselves from the side of the boat and leapt nimbly across onto the buoy. These were 'buoy jumpers' and they were undertaking an exacting and possibly hazardous task. Watching from the forecastle deck beneath the flight deck, I marvelled at the fact that they had not already ended up in the water, given the heavy decoration of trailing brown weed and multi-coloured guano covering the buoy.

The boat backed off a few yards to one side and the grey bow of the ship moved slowly towards them, casting a dark shadow as the sun was obscured. The ship eventually came to a standstill with the raked bow only a few feet above the buoy jumpers. A rope was lowered through the hawse pipe, followed by a steel wire hawser. The rope was grabbed by the buoy jumpers, passed through the iron ring on the top of the buoy, tied to the 'eye' on the end of the hawser, which was then hauled back up through the hawse pipe. With this 'bridle' securing the ship to the buoy, the heavy anchor cable was paid out until it hung at the level of the buoy ring. One of the sailors sitting astride the buoy fished in his satchel and hefted up a large steel shackle, passing it carefully through the last link in the anchor cable and the buoy ring before hammering in the shackle pin and hopping back into the boat. All of this took only a few minutes before everyone was allowed to relax with the ship now safely secured to its mooring buoy.

As the dockyard tugs backed off, the main broadcast blared out over the decks. "D'ye hear there. Stand down from Harbour Stations. Watch on deck stand by to receive the fuelling lighter, port side aft. No smoking throughout the ship." The reason for moving away from the jetty and out to a buoy was now securing alongside the ship. This was a fuel lighter, provided to enable the carrier to take on 'avgas', the high octane volatile fuel required for the Squadron of S2F Grumman Trackers. We had already been topped up with 'avcat', the fuel used by the gas turbine engined helicopters and Skyhawk fighter-bombers. As this fuel was about as benign as paraffin it posed no real risk but the local port authorities were not prepared to contemplate the risk posed by the cargo of high octane petrol which was now arriving. Several remarks from my colleagues reminded me that we were all going to live within a few feet of this volatility for several months. Clearly we were more expendable than the Sydney waterfront.

Once the fuel lighter had been secured alongside and had started pumping fuel, a wooden accommodation ladder was lowered down the starboard side and a series of launches and tenders appeared and started shuttling between the ship and shore. The last of the party guests were being taken off, as packages, boxes, crates of food came on board and other people came and went. A little later on, as the sunshine was being replaced by late afternoon shadows, one particular boatload included Ernie one of our young Squadron sub-lieutenants who was also a Vietnam veteran.

Ernie was generally known within the squadron as 'Wordsworth' because of his habit, when full of booze, of hopping up on the nearest chair or table and reciting long and accurate passages from Shakespeare's plays or from many of the classical poets. Clearly highly intelligent with a powerful retentive memory, he might have been more suited to a career as a classical actor. But he was a junior officer with a powerful thirst and a weakness for joining any likely scheme hatched by his colleagues, usually being the one who was caught out when the scheme failed.

There was no need for me to be informed when officers left the ship and I was unaware that Ernie had gone ashore until I was called down to the gangway later that evening to take a shore telephone call.

Telephone calls when the ship was secured to a mooring buoy were only possible because a telephone cable was laid across the harbour bottom to a connector on the buoy. A telephone cable from the ship was then connected to the terminal. The system was vulnerable to all sorts of communication breaching problems and our particular telephone connection was no exception.

The ratings on duty at a big ship's gangway usually consist of a quartermaster – a leading seaman, assisted by a boatswain's mate and sometimes a side boy to do the fetching and carrying. As I arrived I noticed that the Officer of the Watch was not present, presumably doing rounds, I thought, or possibly checking on the ship's mooring situation from the Bridge. Gangway watchkeepers spend a lot of time doing very little and they either look bored and disgruntled, or if something has happened to brighten up their lives or amuse them, often at the expense of someone else, they begin to look unduly happy and cheerful. This lot looked delighted.

As I arrived, the duty midshipman moved out of the shadows and saluted me. His face was also decorated with a stupid grin. The quartermaster was holding out the telephone and I took it. I held it to my ear and bellowed into the hissing and crackling static *"Melbourne* Officer of the Day!" A faint voice penetrated some of the static and I heard "police, drunk, traffic" and – I thought, "riot". Thus began a ten-minute session of alternately bellowing into the phone and then straining to hear the response. I was crouched over the phone, facing the steel bulkhead with my free hand clamped over my disengaged ear in a vain attempt to shut out the intrusive noises of the ship which, when accustomed, faded into the background, but now served to make a difficult conversation even more so. I felt, rather than saw, the gangway team edging closer to me, anxious not to lose any of the entertainment value.

As my tortured telephone call continued, a boat came alongside and a few officers followed by a group of ratings, trudged up the swaying accommodation ladder and saluted before disappearing into the bowels of the ship. The quartermaster had to break off from his eavesdropping to salute the officers, check identity cards and return station cards to the ratings before they went forward. The returnees left a brief waft of beer and cigarettes behind them before they moved off. The quartermaster moved closer to resume his interest, while relative quiet descended around the gangway. By this time I had established several things. Firstly, the Sydney police had someone from the ship's company in custody. Secondly, not only were they willing to hand the individual back to the ship but they were very keen to do so. Thirdly, whatever their problems were, they were continuing. Fourthly, 817 Squadron was mentioned. This galvanised me into activity. Even in adversity, in every squadron it was axiomatic that you look after your own. Whoever it was, I wanted him back – and as quickly as possible.

I asked the policeman on the phone to hold on – that is to say, I bellowed into the phone and hoped he understood. I then sent the midshipman off to fetch the 817 Squadron Duty Officer as quickly as he could and told the quartermaster to summon the Duty Regulating Petty Officer and the 'standby' Shore Patrol. Within three or four minutes they had all arrived and I shouted my final instructions into the phone concluding with "Got that?" without really waiting for the answer.

Another tender was arriving alongside, discharging three or four returning libertymen and, anticipating nicely, the quartermaster called down to the side boy on the accommodation ladder platform "Hold that boat!" I despatched the Squadron Duty Officer with instructions to get the possible miscreant back on board, to sign nothing and to stand back while allowing his petty officer to lead the shore patrol, now looking impressive in their white belts and gaiters, and carrying big nightsticks.

It was some time around midnight before I had enough information to piece together the full story. Ernie had been dragooned into the wardroom party as an additional host and in this capacity he had been exceptionally successful, becoming towards the end of the party, what might have been termed 'the life and soul' of the declining rump of revellers. After the last of the ship's officers had left for the move out to the buoy and the last stragglers among the guests had gone, Ernie had taken a light lunch and drifted off for a little doze in his cabin. This had lasted until about six, when he had re-emerged, taken a refreshing shower before changing into mess undress (evening) uniform and returning to the wardroom for an early supper. Before eating he had paused for a few 'sharpeners' in the bar. A shared bottle of wine over supper had further boosted his enthusiasm as well as his blood alcohol content. By now in a distinctly mellow frame of mind he had followed his companions into one of the shore-going boats, largely to conclude a vigorous debate that he had become involved in with his friends. The boat arrived at the jetty, the passengers disembarked and the debate continued while the boat cast off and chugged back out in the direction of the ship. The party gradually dispersed and Ernie, being the only officer wearing uniform, waited patiently for the boat to return. Unfortunately the boat's crew had been stood down at that point for their own supper break and consequently there was a gap in the boat schedule of about an hour and a half.

Ernie began to get bored on his own on the jetty and with no sign of any boats he decided to amuse himself by going for a little walk. An officer in evening dress uniform was an unusual sight in the centre of Sydney and inevitably, Ernie fell into conversation with some strollers taking the evening air. This led to some entertainment in a bar then a visit to another bar, and then another, each one getting closer to the city centre. About nine o'clock the party broke up and a slightly befuddled Ernie decided it was time to return to the ship. As he was attempting to engage a taxi, the already heavy traffic in the Kings Cross centre of Sydney had become even more snarled up. Ernie's stationary taxi was adding to the confusion and it occurred to Ernie, always a helpful soul, that he could resolve, or at least ease the developing situation by taking charge and doing a little traffic direction.

This was the situation encountered by the first police patrol when they were summoned to sort out the traffic gridlock, complete with a few minor accidents and several angry motorists, surrounding a small smartly uniformed naval officer waving his arms around in an attempt to resolve the chaos.

Tempers flared, Ernie tried even harder to help, and arrests were made. This included Ernie, who was dragged away and thrown into the back of one of several police vans to be despatched to the Central Sydney Police Station.

The usual practice of the police in circumstances where numbers of people had suddenly come into their custody, was to give them time to dry out and either let them out with a stern warning or line them up for the magistrates in the morning. Noting

Ernie's appearance the duty sergeant decided almost as soon as he saw him that he would be released whenever he could be expected to return safely to his ship. That was before the riot.

Ernie was one among several men who were deeply aggrieved at their sudden incarceration and as they bounced their frustration off each other their feelings of aggression, with accompanying noise, grew. Others joined in and within the hour there was a full scale riot taking place in the 'tank' – the main large communal cell in the police station. Ernie had deployed all of his remaining powers of leadership and persuasion to calm the squabbling, scuffling occupants of the large cell but in so doing had found himself hailed as the leader of the dominant group who then, by aggression and threat, absorbed the other disparate groups and began to direct their ire towards their captors. Rising to the occasion with the intention of calming the volatile atmosphere, Ernie had inadvertently become the leading light in this incipient rebellion. Observing that the disturbance showed every indication of getting out of hand, the custody sergeant surmised correctly that the separation of Ernie, the leader, from the rest, the led, might quieten the situation down. This indeed proved to be the case but largely because most of the detainees had simply run out of steam. As the cell door clanged shut behind a remarkably meek and co-operative Ernie, some of his troops were already lapsing into sleep. The sergeant's hastily assembled snatch squad seemed disappointed that they had faced no aggression as they withdrew still smacking the long truncheons into the palms of their open hands and trying to look hard. The sergeant, with commendable goodwill towards the Royal Australian Navy determined to get rid of Ernie as quickly as he could, but this time under naval escort, back to his ship.

When Ernie returned on board his status within the squadron reached new heights. He was a hero to the naturally rebellious streak that lurked under the disciplined exterior of the young

Australians who comprised the junior cadre of the squadron. The story grew as it spread through the ship. It was said that Ernie had formed and led a protest movement within the city. Ernie had broken out of jail. Ernie had personally accepted the surrender of the entire New South Wales Police Force – and so it developed as it went around the ship.

I had intended to do my best to keep Ernie's Sydney adventure under wraps when he returned in the early hours of the morning, or at least to keep it within the squadron. However, my good intentions were stillborn. Being naturally gregarious, Ernie had entertained his escort all the way back with lurid and conflicting accounts of his adventures so that by the time the petty officer and his escorts arrived on board, they couldn't wait to tell their mates. The fact that Ernie was an officer made the tale even more interesting and it established the birth of a legend that was to follow Ernie throughout the cruise – and beyond.

Another difficulty in my attempts to downplay the story was that the police had felt it necessary to send an accompanying report by hand of the petty officer rather than the Squadron Duty Officer. The report concluded with a recommendation in the strongest terms that when *HMAS Melbourne* next returned to Sydney, Ernie should be detained on board, for his own good, not forgetting the corporate blood pressure of the Sydney Police Force.

Nothing happened before the ship sailed the next morning but as soon as the 'pipe' came for Special Sea Duty-men to stand down a message was conveyed via the Squadron Duty Officer that the Boss, me and Ernie were required to assemble in the 'Commander's' cabin. I assumed that we were not being invited for drinks to celebrate the ship's successful departure, but Ernie seemed unfazed.

44

I was invited somewhat peremptorily to wait outside the Executive Officer's cabin so I joined an expanding group of most of the officers and ratings who had been on duty the day before. The Boss and Ernie disappeared inside the cabin and raised voices were heard, or perhaps more accurately, one raised voice and others more subdued. Eventually a cross-looking Boss emerged with Ernie trailing behind, both disappearing quickly down the adjacent ladder to the deck below, in the general direction of the briefing room – or perhaps the Boss's cabin for yet another 'bollicking' for poor Ernie. I came to the conclusion that my services were no longer required so I clattered down the ladder as well.

As I strolled back towards the briefing room several thoughts chased one another through my head. First I found it a bit odd that I had been given a ship's duty to do and yet I had not even met the 'Commander' – the ship's Executive Officer, nor for that matter had any other squadron officer seen or met any of the ship's senior officers – other than Ernie and the Boss, that is.

Chapter 3

Newspapers

I had been irritated, not so much by Ernie's unfortunate adventure as by the reaction of the senior officers. It was a tiny thing but being invited to stand and wait outside the Commander's cabin as though in some way I had been responsible for Ernie rather than being the unfortunate Officer of the Day, left me feeling aggrieved and irritated. However my irritation was quickly displaced by another curious problem that I began to mull over. I was aware that it was the practice of the Royal Navy in those days to send airmail copies of *The Times* to each foreign or commonwealth ship or establishment where British officers were serving on loan or exchange. These papers were sent once or twice a week rather than every day and were always addressed to 'The Senior British Officer'. I had seen these newspapers at the Naval Air Station at Nowra but there were so many British officers serving there that, by common consent, they were all placed in a folder in the wardroom to be read by anyone interested. I wondered whether this routine prevailed onboard the flagship but could find no sign of any British newspapers in the wardroom or the anteroom. Meanwhile we sailed from Sydney.

The next task for the ship was to cruise down the coast and wait for the two fixed-wing squadrons to fly aboard. Since I still had very little to do I thought I would make my way up into the 'island' to see if I could find a place near 'Flyco' to watch the fixed-wing squadrons embark. I joined the elite band known in aircraft carriers as 'the goofers', perched around the 'island' superstructure like hungry crows, most of whom were present in the hope of witnessing a spectacular crash.

In fact after the first hour and the successful embarkation of six of the eight Skyhawks due and four of the six Trackers I became bored and made my way back down the multiple ladders to 'aircrew country'. The engineers and maintenance crews of the two squadrons were of course already on board which meant that the preparation and departure from Nowra was being handled by the appropriate training squadrons. This had evidently slowed down the departure somewhat and had further slowed the reaction to inevitable last minute defects – 'gremlins' – which had become apparent in a few cases.

All six of the serviceable Skyhawks had arrived in impressive style, sweeping down the side of the ship in one echelon before breaking formation to orbit the ship while each aircraft successively descended to pretty impressive landings, catching the middle arrester wire and then quickly taxiing out of the way to make room for the next one. The much bigger twin-propeller Trackers were not so fortunate. Five of them turned up in a nice 'V' formation for a flypast before slipping neatly into echelon, while aircraft peeled off from the back of the echelon individually to approach the deck for a landing. The first two landed without incident but the third and fourth aircraft both 'bolted', each going into a wide port-hand circuit to try again while the fifth aircraft, the formation leader slipped in and completed a workmanlike landing, catching the last wire. The two 'bolters' followed each other round in a very wide circuit before making their second attempt. One after another they each bolted a second time, raising the collective interest of the 'goofers' and producing a worried frown on the face of their

Squadron C.O., who was already on board and watching from 'Flyco'.

One of the aircraft turned left into another circuit while the other one climbed and turned to the right, presumably at the direction of 'Flyco', to orbit above the ship. I watched the lower Tracker as he entered a distant downwind leg and I could imagine the nerves and sweat rising inside the cockpit as the enormity of failure, seemingly in front of the whole world engulfed the pilot, making his subsequent attempts to land even more problematic. He need not have worried. Every aviator watching was willing both aircraft to succeed and if any of the 'fish-heads' (non-aviating sailors) had any derogatory feelings they wisely kept them to themselves. At the third attempt the lead aircraft of the pair achieved an almost perfect touchdown, neatly catching the centre wire as though he had been doing it all his life. In fact it was his first embarked deck landing. A small cheer echoed around the 'goofers'.

The last Tracker had seen the successful landing in front of him from his orbit a thousand feet above the ship. By the time he turned and had descended back down to 'circuit' level before entering the final approach position, the aircraft in front had folded its wings and was already on the lift, on its way to the hangar. As the lift had yet to return to the deck, the approaching aircraft was given "continue" as opposed to "land" in response to his 'Finals' call over the radio. He had reached a position on the approach about three or four hundred yards short of the deck before the lift was locked back in place and the call to "land" went out from 'Flyco'. By this time the pilot was already increasing power and raising his wing flaps to abandon the approach and climb away. The tension caused in the cockpit was obviously too much and after a short conversation between the pilot and his Boss in Flyco it was decided that the aircraft should return to Nowra to give the crew time to relax before accompanying the last, still unserviceable, aircraft out to the ship later in the day. The planeguard helicopter was swiftly recalled to the ship, the 'goofers' disappeared and we all trooped off for lunch.

I devoted the next few hours to continuing my search for the airmail editions of *The Times*. Concluding that there must be other British officers on board I went in search of them – or rather in search of the Master at Arms who should be able to tell me from his personnel and accommodation lists how many of my countrymen were on board, who they were and where I could find them.

Warrant Officer Master at Arms Crispin was very helpful. I learned that there were three other British officers on board, a seaman lieutenant, a supply branch lieutenant and a Special Duties engineering sub-lieutenant. This officer was much older than the others, having been promoted from the lower deck to what was generally called SD (meaning Special Duties) status. There was also a Chief Air Engineering Artificer and a Petty Officer Communications Yeoman. It was quickly established from the list of ship's officers that each of these officers was substantially junior to me in either rank or seniority. I was the Senior British Officer, so armed with this information I set off to find the Ship's Postman and collect my mail.

I was not so well received when I eventually tracked down the postman in his little office – a space between bits of machinery for which no other use had been found. He was sitting on a chair in front of what looked like a largish homemade desk. Behind him was a huge rack of pigeonholes each one representing a mess or in one or two cases an individual. Most of the racks were empty, except two adjacent racks marked 'Admiral' and 'Captain'.

"Hello," I said. "I'm Lieutenant Holt and I'm looking for some official mail that has been sent to me."

"It'll all be in the wardroom, sir," he said, hardly looking up.

"I don't think so," I persisted staring pointedly at the adjacent pigeonholes for the Captain and Admiral, each of which seemed to have what looked like several tightly folded newspapers with the texture of tissue paper. "I think those are mine over there," I said. He got up, looking very tall and thin.

"No," he said, quite firmly, "those are despatches for the Captain and the Admiral". If he really believed this, I thought, he was in the running for 'Idiot of the Fleet'.

Smiling, I said, "Could I see one of those, please?" Reluctantly he turned and stretched out his thin gangling arm to take down one of the folded newspapers. He held it almost reverently. I leaned over the half-door entrance and peered towards it. "What does it say on the address?" I asked, still preserving my air of matey friendliness. He moved slightly towards me while peering at the address on the wrapping label. This allowed me the opportunity to lean over and surprise him by lifting the bundle out of his hand. He wanted to hang on to it but didn't fancy a tugging match which might have damaged what he still believed to be the Captain's correspondence.

"Look," I said. "There, see, it's addressed to the Senior British Officer, *HMAS Melbourne*! That's me," I ended triumphantly.

"No sir," he responded doggedly with a rather fixed expression appearing on his face. "That's mail for the Captain."

"OK," I said. "You win. I'll go up to the Bridge and ask the Captain what he is doing with my mail, sent to me by my government." The fixed, grim expression turned slowly to one of horror. I had suggested a course that would, he thought, bode disaster.

I thought that an attempt to leap the desk and seize the newspaper bundles would go down badly and give the Commander another opportunity to demonstrate his power over junior officers, so I went back to my cabin to consider my next move. On the way I thought it prudent to drop in at the briefing room to see what was new.

The Squadron Duty Officer was Jack – a young sub-lieutenant on his second deployment in the carrier and therefore less likely to drop the squadron into any of the onboard pitfalls awaiting the unwary. As I arrived he was conducting a sort of ballet dance between the bank of sound-powered phones on the bulkhead, the big roller blackboard at the front of the room and the Perspex display boards showing aircraft serviceability, officers' locations, telephone numbers, flying programmes and other bits and pieces of information essential to producing the right men and the right aircraft in the correct place at a precise time – and ensuring that they are all capable of meeting the task imposed on them.

He stepped back from the blackboard, chalk and duster in hand, and admired his handiwork. Satisfied with what he saw he glanced across at me, inclined his head and said, "Coffee?" Since it is almost a criminal offence to refuse such an offer in the world of naval aviators, I said, "Thanks" and settled myself into one of the chairs in the front row. At the back of the room, the only other occupant placed his paperback novel carefully on the flight planning bench, slid off his tall stool and moved towards the coffee makings.

"I'll get it, sir," he said. "NATO standard, sir?" he asked, looking towards me.

"No sugar," I replied.

"Gotcha."

I turned back towards Jack. I decided to explore a growing theory. "Do you know the name of the Captain, Jack?" I asked.

"He is the Godfather," said Jack.

"Yes, but what's his name?" I persisted

"I am not allowed to know his name sir," said Jack, with mock formality. "I am only a squadron sub-lieutenant. Such things are above me."

"OK," I said. "What's the name of the Admiral?" I sipped my coffee.

"He is the other Godfather," replied Jack, beginning to enjoy himself.

"He must have a name," I said.

"I have heard it whispered within the darker passageways in this ship that with his friends he may answer to the strange name of 'FOCAF'. Jack was confirming to me something that I already suspected. That was the remoteness of the senior officers in this ship, which to some extent reflected a pattern throughout the Navy. FOCAF was in fact, an acronym – and meant 'Flag Officer Commanding Australian Fleet'. We each focussed on our coffee and the conversation died.

When I thought about this attitude years later, which was typified by what I learnt from Jack that afternoon and was widespread among the embarked squadrons, I formed the view that the stilted set of relationships existing within that ship may have had much to do with a series of events which collectively gave the ship its unlucky reputation.

Certainly my own experience bore out much of what I had heard. In the Royal Navy I was used to a cohesive spirit within the wardroom with captains and other senior officers who not only knew their officers and men but who went to great lengths to ensure that their men knew them and recognised their humanity as well as their power and status. Opportunities were taken to invite officers to senior ratings' messes, the Captain would invite groups of officers to dine with him and hospitality would be returned from the wardroom. The pattern extended all the way back to Nelson and it was a good formula for developing an effective team and could be described as being 'all of one company'. This was very far from my experience onboard *Melbourne*.

I never really met any of the Commanders who headed the various departments within the ship, with the exception of the occasional very brief duty directive from the Executive Commander and some unmemorable platitudes from the CAG. I never actually spoke with the Captain or the Admiral even when I tried to help with Bridge watchkeeping and I don't recall any squadron officer being invited to lunch or a drink with either of those two. Not only did most of us not know or care who they were, they didn't know or care about us. Our line of contact went as far as the Squadron Boss and stopped there. This was an unfortunate state of affairs but in my case, I was the Senior British Officer, the representative of my Service and my country and the insult of being ignored by these important people went further than just me.

I finished my coffee, rinsed the mug in the sink at the back of the room and nodded thanks to the Duty Aircrewman who was taking a break from his paperback by tidying up the 'coffee boat'. I wandered back out into the passageway, my mind already focussing once again on the question of how to get access to my newspapers. Jack was talking loudly and earnestly into one telephone while holding the other in his hand. A problem had arisen with the need to exchange an unserviceable aircraft on the flight deck with its serviceable replacement from the hangar. The aircraft handlers who would need to conduct the aircraft to and from the lift and on the flight deck were apparently not playing ball.

By the time I reached my cabin I had already formed an outline plan of action. I would add to the already copious flow of paper around the ship by producing my own memorandum. As I prepared to draft this I noticed yet another sheet of paper which had been slipped under my door. I was requested to contact the Master at Arms as soon as convenient.

I was confident that I knew what the Master at Arms wished to discuss and although I didn't want to get myself on the wrong side of such an important personage within the ship's company, I thought it would do no harm to make him wait a bit while I put my plan into practice.

It had already become apparent to me that this ship, more than others, functioned on the river of memoranda produced by all and sundry and used for directing instructions on everything from how to take a shower without using too much water to who was allowed to wear what, when going ashore.

I sat down at my fold-down desk, tore a sheet of paper from some damage control instructions and began to draft Memo Number 1 from The Senior British Officer, *HMAS Melbourne*. I set out an address list starting with the other three RN officers, in strict order of seniority, followed by the two senior ratings. I added the Master at Arms and Ship's Postman, finishing off with the Captain's Secretary, Commander's Office and Wardroom Chief Steward. I wrote: *'Airmail copies of the London Times newspaper are routinely posted by the British Ministry of Defence to all British Officers serving in Loan or Exchange appointments overseas. Where there is more than one British officer serving in a ship or establishment the Senior British officer in that ship or establishment is to arrange appropriate distribution among other British officers and ratings, ensuring that all such personnel are afforded a proper opportunity to see the newspaper in a timely fashion.*

With immediate effect, the Airmail London Times will be collected from the Ship's Post Office after each onboard delivery, by the Senior British Officer or an officer designated by him. Distribution for each newspaper will be as follows: Lt Arthur, Lt Rudd, Sub Lt Hill, CPO Delany and PO James. Thereafter, the newspaper will be placed in the wardroom. Old copies will be available from the SBO after the distribution is complete.'

I was confident that this might well be construed as poking a finger in the eye of authority but my fine sense of justice had been disturbed. The British taxpayer was sending these newspapers around the world for British sailors. They were not going to be taken as an unearned perk by local senior officers.

The next part of the plan was more complex. I needed a typewriter, a master reproduction sheet for use with the messy Gestetner duplicating machine and finally, a means of delivery to the key recipients by third party.

The afternoon was rolling on by the time I located a typewriter which was not in use. I found this in the tiny Squadron Office but the office was occupied by the Air Engineer's Writer, a Leading Air Engineering Mechanic who had done a week's course in office management, filing and typewriting. The office was shared, on a time basis, with one of the junior aircrewmen whose additional duties included the production of Flying Programmes, Squadron Daily Orders and letters on behalf of the Boss. He had not done the 'Office Writers' Course' since officialdom did not recognise the need for his existence but in fact his natural talent enabled him to produce better results than his engineering counterpart. The office was only really big enough for one of them at a time and they were in the process of changing occupancy, accompanied by the usual mild banter common among sailors. I waited.

As the Air Engineer's Writer departed down the passageway, clutching an armful of box files, dockets and paper, the new incumbent looked up expectantly. As Squadron Executive Officer one of my few duties entailed the production of routine orders and other bits of paper, not including the Flying Programme, which remained the prerogative of the Senior Pilot. My predecessor in this role had determined on a quiet life with as few distractions as possible but I had already introduced myself to our office scribe, taking the line that I wasn't going to interfere with the very good job he was doing but that I was there to help, had one or two ideas that might be useful and was always available if needed. We had started off on a good footing and I was about to capitalise on that.

Taking the bull by the horns, I leaned into the miniature office, placed my handwritten draft on the typewriter in front of the young aircrewman and said:

"That's worth a beer, Dusty, if you can knock out a dozen copies of that for me before you do Daily Orders."

56

"I've got to do the Flying Programme as well, sir," Dusty replied, eyeing me quizzically.

"Not much on for us tomorrow – just some planeguard and a bit of dunking," I lied. Actually I had no idea of what the Flying Programme might contain. "Anyway," I added, "it won't be ready for hours yet." He gave in, grinned, said, "I fancy the Tuborg and reached under the desk for a Gestetner master sheet.

Beer was good currency because for much of the time at sea the Australian Navy was dry except for occasional 'beer issues' promulgated by signal, and even then alcohol, mostly beer, was strictly rationed for junior ratings. "Good on yer," I said as I strode away working out how to smuggle an unopened can of Tuborg lager out of the wardroom without attracting attention. I need not have worried, a beer issue was announced a few days later and clearly, many blind eyes were being turned towards officers walking off with unopened cans of beer and lager.

I waited in my cabin for half an hour or so, using the time to glance through the pile of official-looking paper which had been making its way under my door – most of which I assessed as unnecessary or incomprehensible rubbish – before I set off back to the Squadron Office. Dusty had been as good as his word. His hands were now smudged with black printing ink, the inevitable product of trying to deal with the filthy, inky, Gestetner machine, as he handed me my now neatly typed bundle of memos. The next task should be relatively straightforward. I took the copies back to my cabin and wrote the name of an addressee on each one before taking four of them, folded and pinned, back to the briefing room where I popped them into the internal mail. I then hung about to make sure I was put on to several flying sorties the next day so I would be justifiably unavailable to any irritated Master at Arms, postman, or anyone else who might take exception to my handiwork.

Actually I heard nothing more on the subject but the rolled bundles of tissue paper *Times* started to arrive regularly, stuffed into the 'H' slot in the wardroom letter racks.

Chapter 4

Work-Up Training

Eventually, when we had embarked all of the Carrier Air Group, we steamed south down the picturesque coast of New South Wales to do some initial work-up training for the Air Group. To make things as easy as possible it was decided that the carrier should do much of the embarked flying within the confines of Jervis Bay. As the bay was nearly ten miles long from north to south, *Melbourne* could stay in the bay and get on to a flying course for long enough to launch or recover a pair of jets providing there was a good wind in the right direction, yet be able to slip outside the bay if conditions were suitably benign. In this way the maximum amount of flying could be achieved in the available time. It also meant that spares could be sourced almost instantly from Nowra which was only ten minutes' flying time away.

For us in the helicopter squadron, embarked operations seemed little different from shore-side flying, with the possible exception that aircraft moves from hangar to deck and start-up times had to be observed strictly, the alternative being deep embarrassment at best and multiple bollickings, stoppage of leave, extra duties and absolute ignominy at worst. We were, in fact, kept quite busy during this period because in addition to our own routine training sorties we were generally required to provide a 'planeguard' helicopter, stationed off the port bow for fixed-wing launches and moved back to the port quarter for recoveries, so that in the event of a fixed-wing accident the helicopter crew could be immediately on hand to recover survivors. Although in bigger exercises a destroyer or frigate would be sometimes appointed to act as planeguard, the hierarchy of *Melbourne* tended to shy away from this, having previously rammed and sunk the planeguard destroyer on no less than two occasions in the past. For the helicopter crews 'planeguarding' was incredibly boring work and not inclined to improve the temperament of the pilot selected (often as retribution for misdemeanours) for this duty.

A last minute decision based on a falling wind and a nervous met officer led to the carrier moving out of Jervis Bay in order to carry out some intensive deck landing practice for the Skyhawks. The ship weighed anchor and got under way immediately after the decision had been taken at the morning briefing, and somehow this decision led to another which was to bring forward the Skyhawks' deck landing practice. Consequently there was an earlier and more protracted requirement for a planeguard helicopter. As usual, and unfortunately, a great deal of time passed while the ship was weighing anchor and manoeuvring towards the opening from the bay to the ocean, before the officers in 'Flyco' decided to let the rest of the floating world in on their secret.

Since sudden demands for the use of a helicopter were not uncommon we in the helicopter squadron had a well worked-up routine for such occasions. Each day a Squadron Duty Officer was nominated and, when we were at sea a duty crew was also nominated, primarily to take on tasks not foreseen when planning the squadron flying programme. By long-standing tradition in the Royal Navy and all the Commonwealth navies, such duties would last twenty-four hours and would be handed on to the next duty personnel at eight o'clock each morning.

The ship had been at anchor overnight and routines had been relaxed, onboard bars were open and, in the case of the wardroom, had done brisk business. By the start of the briefing, the nominated Duty Crew pilot, Peter Archer, had reached the conclusion that during the previous evening he had celebrated to excess and was now somewhat hung over. He was distinctly unhappy about the prospect of having later to spend several hours sweating under the cockpit Perspex watching jet jockeys zoom past. In attempting to overcome this difficulty his befuddled brain came up with a possible solution. If he could persuade the off-going Squadron Duty Officer, who was already kitted up in flying overalls, to take his place as pilot of the Squadron Duty Crew on the basis of an offer to reciprocate a few days later he could slink away and all would be well.

As the morning briefing came to an end he made his offer to the now off-watch Duty Officer. This was sub-lieutenant Henry, also known as 'Billy' Budd. To his surprise, Peter's proposal was accepted after only a brief discussion. During the discussion it was noted that the jet jockeys would be flying during the afternoon and that the Duty Crew would be free during the forenoon. Billy concluded that he was a winner in the deal because he would have a fairly free morning and be well set up for the planned session of early evening and night flying later that day.

The decision to take the ship out of Jervis Bay to operate offshore meant that all of the day's programmes and plans for every department were thrown into disarray. This meant that not only was the deck landing practice for the Skyhawks being brought forward to the forenoon but in effect, as was shortly to become apparent, it also meant 'begin the exercise immediately'.

The first indication that the intentions of the Command had changed came in the form of a 'pipe' from the flight deck and hangar broadcast, which boomed out "Range the planeguard". In fact this order occurred only about six minutes after Peter had arranged to swap duties with 'Billy' Budd, so that Peter would enjoy what he had hoped would be a quieter morning including a late leisurely breakfast in the Aircrew Refreshment Bar, otherwise known as Wardroom Two.

Billy, also unaware of the change in plans had assumed that he had time to visit the heads and prepare himself and his crew without undue haste. No money had changed hands between the two but promises of multiple drinks had been included in the deal.

Billy heard the 'pipe' instructing the planeguard helicopter to be ranged just as he was settling into the essential business of the day in the 'heads'. Before the implication of the broadcast order had sunk into Billy's head, the broadcast boomed out again "Scramble the planeguard." This was really not necessary because the A4 Skyhawk pilots were only halfway through their briefing and, as we 'chopper pukes' would have it, they had yet to preen and pose in front of any mirror they passed as well as checking that they had sufficient resources to cope with any diversion ashore. Nevertheless, the order had been issued and the use of the word "scramble" meant get airborne as quickly as possible.

Billy completed his ablutions as quickly as he could, flushed the lavatory and set off fast for the flight deck, intending to call at the Aircrew Locker Room to pick up his Mae West and 'bone dome' on the way.

Moving about inside a large operational warship is not always straightforward. Painting, cleaning, repairing, damage control exercises and Captain's rounds can erect significant barriers to easy movement.

And so it was for Billy. As he made his hurried way from 'Officer's Country' near the stern towards the squadron area he first encountered a heavy watertight door with two steel 'clips' rammed home to keep the door shut. He immediately attacked the clips securing the steel door, all the while standing on the 'painting in progress' sign which had detached itself from the top of the door and now rested on the deck – face down. He heaved mightily on the top, then the lower clip, nervous energy lending him strength. The clips gave way to his heaving and the door was flung open. Billy leapt through the doorway on to the shiny wet grey deck paint. His second step tipped the paint pot over and resulted in loud imprecations from the deck painters. Horrified, Billy stepped back through the doorway aiming for an alternative route up the 'Cabin Flat' ladder to the deck above, trailing a line of grey footprints along the otherwise gleaming vinyl tiles. On the next deck, work was taking place on the air conditioning system but Billy charged past, desperate now to reach the crew room and the flight deck.

While Billy was trying to reach the flight deck, Peter had been intercepted by the Squadron Boss who wasted little energy in pointing out to Peter, whose name remained on the Duty Crew List, that he was already in deep shit and a failure to appear on the flight deck, or preferably in the aircraft cockpit would result in him being drowned in it.

The two hapless young pilots emerged together from the flight deck Control Office in the base of the 'island', both were now panicked and aiming to climb into the same seat in the same aircraft.

As they reached the helicopter ranged on the after operating spot, the flight deck broadcast roared into action, issuing a florid and extensive bollicking to both young men, ending in the casting of considerable doubt on the intellectual capacity and the parentage of each young officer, to the obvious delight of every sailor within range of the powerful speakers. As an afterthought they were both invited to call on the Carrier Air Group Commander – probably, we thought, not for the purpose of sharing a beer.

A paint-spattered Billy heaved himself into the aircraft while Peter, with an even bigger headache, slunk off to find somewhere to avoid both the Squadron Boss and the Air Boss and to try to concoct a plausible story. An impossible task as it turned out.

By the time the squadron assembled for the briefing preceding the dusk and night-flying programme each pilot had suffered several very uncomfortable interviews and had been deprived of a considerable amount of their future liberty. Worse still they were the butt of raucous humour throughout the Air Group.

Fate decreed two further inconsistencies to fuel the wordless acrimony which now dominated the relationship between the former friends. The first was that each pilot blamed the other for his misfortune. The second was that a stroke of incredible incompetence on behalf of the Senior Pilot led to both officers being included in the same crew for the second sortie of the evening.

The sortie was a straightforward 'night dunking' exercise. This entailed flying the helicopter around in a pattern to simulate the tracking of a submarine, using the aircraft's dipping sonar. The aircraft were to operate from the ship at anchor inside Jervis Bay and to carry out the entire exercise within the bay. With the usual formalities completed without much communication, the crew, two pilots, and the tactical battle fighting and navigating team of observer and aircrewman sonar operator, headed out on to the flight deck to do the external walk round of the aircraft, man up and get airborne. Even innocent remarks and smiling friendliness from the deck crews served to intensify the deep embarrassment of the two young pilots and the atmosphere of near hatred which fluttered between them.

The big helicopter rose into a low hover, moved to the left following the marshaller's wands, eased the nose down and climbed away into the evening sky. The crew settled into the standard routine, flying at a height of two hundred feet and a speed of ninety knots. The observer in the aircraft cabin passed directions up to the pilots as they approached the point where they were to begin the first automatic transition from a hundred and fifty feet down to a stable hover at forty feet above the sea level. The aircraft was lined up into wind and speed reduced to sixty knots before the button was pressed to begin the run 'down the slope' to achieve a steady hover using the radio altimeter to control height and the Doppler System to control horizontal movement.

By the time the aircraft had established a hover, the sun had set and the slightly overcast sky was darkening. The order "Lower the body" was given and the aircrewman operated the high-speed winch to lower the sonar set into the sea. As the exercise was primarily for the benefit of the pilots the winch was stopped when the sonar body had reached a depth of about sixty feet. At this point a switch was selected so that the aircraft hover point was related to the position of the sonar cable rather than the Doppler system.

All of this and the routine checking of engine gauges necessitated quite a bit of communication between the pilots. This began as terse monosyllables but gradually included a level of sneering sarcasm until the pilot in the left-hand seat, who was not monitoring the controls at the time, threw his arm backward to strike his colleague across the front of his face. The victim's hands flew from the controls as he sought to retaliate. A struggle ensued between the two pilots and blows were exchanged as the aircraft lurched back and forth just above the sea surface. The terrified back-seat crew raised the sonar body back into the aircraft and when this happened the aircraft lost its automatic ability to maintain the hover. It went skating off at a tangent swooping and diving towards the sea from a height of only forty feet as the battle in the cockpit continued. The observer was yelling over the intercom but to no effect so in a desperate attempt to get some rational reaction from the front seats he pulled his emergency knife from its holder on the side of his overall trousers and used it to stab at the back of the two pairs of green-clad legs he could see above and in front of him.

Sharp pains from a different direction brought a modicum of sense into the dangerous mayhem. The observer, who was the senior officer in the crew, ordered an immediate return to the ship and it seemed as if shame suddenly replaced the madness that had overcome the two young officers.

When they returned on board, the observer claimed that a defect in the automatic hover system had forced them to return and apart from an exceptionally terse and forthright debriefing, and the application of some plasters to the calves of four legs, nothing more was said about the incident. Interestingly, both pilots left the ship, for different reasons, within the next few weeks. By the time we returned to Nowra some months later the incident had achieved the status of folklore and of course it had expanded dramatically in the telling. Not long before my departure from Australia I was engaged in conversation by a young lieutenant at a Nowra Wardroom party who, seeking to impress a Pommie as to the boldness and fearlessness of his peers, described to me how in the dead of night, while hovering over Jervis Bay, the pilots had fought over a lady's honour and one pilot had forced the other out of the cockpit and down on to the main wheel strut before the observer had intervened by grabbing the aggressor by the legs and restraining him. I asked sceptically if the fleeing pilot had unbuckled his five-point seat harness in order to climb outside. My companion wandered off to consider the matter.

Chapter 5

Old Saucer Eyes

It was during this initial work up period that I met 'Old Saucer Eyes'. We were still operating in the Jervis Bay area, moving outside the bay to operate the Skyhawk fighter-bombers and then returning, usually to anchor, within the bay to fly the helicopters in their anti-submarine, dipping sonar role.

My crew was launched as part of a trio of helicopters that were to simulate a search for a non-existent submarine down through the bay. In the event the first aircraft due to take off was declared unserviceable so the remaining two took off together in the late afternoon, each to take the opportunity to exercise the inexperienced co-pilot in the technique required to fly the aircraft down to establish a stable hover – without being able to see the outside world. Normally this would be achieved using 'two stage ambers' – the cockpit windows would be fitted with amber-coloured screens and the pilot under training would wear blue goggles. The combined blue and amber would prevent that pilot from looking outside but would still allow him to see the instruments and controls within the cockpit. But on this occasion, because we would be airborne from just before sunset, through dusk and into night conditions the 'ambers' had been dispensed with and I was relying on my inexperienced co-pilot to be a good boy and just keep his focus of vision inside the cockpit.

These exercises could be quite demanding and stressful for the pilot under training but for the instructor or safety pilot they could become quite boring. I was in the habit of taking over and giving my protégé a break from time to time but otherwise I whiled away the time by keeping an eye on the engine and flying instruments, looking around at the shoreline of the bay, watching to see where the other helicopters were and generally admiring the limited amount of water traffic on a balmy evening. I would interrupt this from time to time by switching off some important system to test my pupil in his recovery technique but as this one was really quite skilled, even this sport failed to ease the boredom.

I glanced yet again at the instruments then at my watch as we sat in the hover with the sonar body lowered forty feet or so below the sea surface. I yawned and casually looked outside, around the bay and then at the water beneath the aircraft. What I saw shook me out of my soporific mood more effectively than sudden immersion under a cold shower.

I was looking at a huge dorsal fin, mostly grey but with a distinct white tip. My mind was catapulted back to the many stories I had listened to since arriving in Australia. The whole coast of Eastern Australia was renowned for its offshore shark population. Shark attacks of one sort or another were regularly reported and, despite its fabulous beaches, not much swimming took place around the edge of Jervis Bay. The shark population within the bay was known to be at least as concentrated as along the rest of the coast and many thought more so in view of the abundant supply of fish. One story told locally and repeated time and again, related to a huge 'White Pointer' shark reckoned to be at least twenty-five feet long, which according to repeated and occasionally boozy tales lived almost permanently within the bay. It was rumoured to have attacked boats, devoured all sorts of things and was generally used to put the frighteners on anyone proposing to go down to the beach.

Whenever I heard any of these stories, which generally seemed to relate to events which had taken place many years ago at some indeterminate time, I always expressed polite interest but flavoured it with extreme scepticism. Now, living and breathing, forty feet below me, was the subject of the legend. I was no longer a sceptic! For several moments I stared, fascinated, out of the cockpit window. Although the sun had set a few minutes before, there was still plenty of light and there could be no doubt of what I was seeing. I tried to judge the height of the fin sticking above the water and concluded that it was at least four possibly five feet. Although no expert on sharks I could clearly see the white tip of the fin. I peered into the water trying to see the body of the fish and I could make out a huge grey shape tailing away in front of and behind the fin. The beast seemed to be circling the cable attached to our sonar body below the surface and I realised at the same time that through the aircraft intercom system I could hear the distinctive ping of our active sonar transmissions.

As I continued to stare, fascinated and horrified, I glanced across at the engine instruments and the thought entered my mind that this would be a very bad place to suffer an engine failure. We were all well trained in how to survive a ditching in the sea but the thought of adding to the adrenalin flow by ending up on the back of the biggest shark within miles was just too much to contemplate. "Raise the body," I ordered intent on clearing out from our present position as quickly as possible.

"But we've only just got here," came over the intercom from the right-hand seat.

"Hang on, we've got something here." I recognised our observer's voice.

"Raise the body," I repeated as I continued to stare at the great grey brute still lazily circling around underneath us.

"No, no, hang on, we've got a contact." Our observer sounded excited. I was distracted by trying to calculate the length of the shark, comparing it with the length of the helicopter fuselage. I reckoned it to be at least twenty-five feet in length and probably nearer to thirty. I realised that we were still in the hover and the sonar body was still in the water.

"Raise the bloody body!" I shouted into the intercom.

"Why?" came the truculent response from the cabin.

"Because we're sitting on top of a bloody great shark and I'd rather be somewhere else," I responded somewhat heatedly.

"Oh," came a chorus from at least two intercom positions. However I was relieved to see that the sonar cable was being raised. I continued to watch the shark, wondering whether he would clamp his teeth onto the large chunk of metal and plastic that was the sonar body, as it passed his nose. He didn't.

We climbed away from the hover, turned and circled back over the position and everyone peered down. There was no sign of the great predator and so after a quick conference we agreed to move to the other end of the bay and do a couple of practice 'transition to the hover' procedures without putting the sonar in the water. Then, to satisfy our combined rising curiosity, I agreed that we should lower the sonar body once more and carry out one all-round passive sweep. There was no sign of the shark but I suppose I was not really expecting to see him (or her?) again.

A couple of days later, the powers that be decided that as many aircrew as possible should carry out a routine survival drill –

called 'Wet Dinghy Drill', before leaving the area. This would involve being flown ashore by helicopter to a temporary landing site near the beach. There we were to be met by a team from the Nowra Survival Section, who would take us out into the bay in groups in their boat. An inflated one-man dinghy would be then launched into the water and the selected victim, dressed in an old flying suit, would leap over the side of the boat and strike out for the dinghy. When this was reached the swimmer would attempt to drag himself face down into the semi-waterlogged dinghy and then squirm around until he was sitting upright, surrounded by wet rubber. Finally he would poke about to find the oral inflation tube and, if he had recovered sufficient breath, he would puff into the tube until he had inflated the floor of the dinghy. There were variations on this routine such as finding and firing off flares or locating the cover and hood, then snuggling down inside the cocoon thus formed – or at least that is what the instructors said.

In fact the main purpose of the drill was to demonstrate to each of us just how exhausting it could be after a ditching to simply find and climb aboard the tiny rubber boat without ending upside down underneath it.

When it came to my turn I realised I was coping with an added complication. I could not shake off the mental image of a huge grey shark with a white-tipped fin lurking just below the surface waiting for his lunch. Putting this image to one side and mentally willing the orange and black dinghy to float towards me, I took a mighty leap out of the boat which would have qualified me for the Air Station long jump team before I even hit the water, and landed with arms and legs already flailing to propel me towards the dinghy as quickly as possible. In a few seconds I shot out of the water, flinging myself face down in the dinghy. A great feeling of relief welled over me. I was safe, old Saucer Eyes wasn't going to get me – unless he had developed a taste for wet rubber.

As I lay, breathless, face down in the dinghy, nose pressed into smelly wet rubber, with my overalls already drying from the hot morning sun I could dimly hear the Petty Officer Survival Instructor lecturing his remaining charges.

"Yeah, fellas, that's the way it should be done. No farting about, as soon as you hit the water go for that bloody dinghy – and go like shit sliding off a shovel." He droned on as I realised with a rising sense of amazement that he was actually talking about me.

****

As I climbed down from the cabin of the helicopter delivering me back on board, my attention was caught by the sight of several ratings heaving a series of heavy blue bags through the screen door in the base of the 'island'. Mail! Every sailor's delight! We had only been away for a few days but I was anxious to discover whether there was any news from home. I squelched across to the door in my sopping kit and instinctively followed the mail into the bowels of the ship. Trailing through the ship's passages in wet gear was likely to produce a multiplicity of sense of humour failures so I made straight for my cabin. I stripped off the wet clothing and dropped the soaking overalls into the washbasin, put on my basic shipboard uniform and set off as quickly as I could for the wardroom. The mail would not be sorted for half an hour or so but I wanted to be in pole position when it arrived.

I was in luck. I spotted the familiar handwriting while it was still in the hand of the steward sorting the letters into their 'pigeonholes'. News from home. Irene had been as good as her word and she must have written the letter almost as soon as she had arrived back from Sydney. It was a short letter. All was well at home, Rebecca seemed to accept that Daddy would be away for a while (in her outlook that meant at least a day) and Spoofy seemed to have decided to stay much closer to home and assume the posture of an alert guard – apart from when he was enjoying his siesta inside the old Holden station wagon. It didn't matter how short the letter was – it was a letter from home.

Chapter 6

Going North

We finished the last of the drills, loaded up with some more stores and then sailed without ceremony out through the narrow entrance of the bay, turned left after travelling five miles or so off the coast and headed north. With the ship running into a convenient headwind, speed was increased to twenty knots and a flight of three Skyhawks was launched to form up and treat the town of Nowra, and the airfield married quarters, to a farewell flypast. By the time they were back on board and had been struck down into the hangar we were already approaching Sydney and our escorting frigates were showing up as blips on the radar.

With the escorts in company and *HMAS Supply*, our stores and fuel support ship rolling along behind, we continued north from the Sydney area and started to repeat much of the work-up, with most of the flying being used to train the escorting frigates. Our route lay just outside the Barrier Reef and the idyllic weather conditions encouraged and intensified the aviation work-up programme. This entailed the continuation of the tradition among all carrier air groups that the fixed-wing people flew throughout daylight and the unlovely helicopters were left with all the night flying – or so it seemed.

Naval Air Squadrons had to be self-contained units, capable of moving from ship to ship or ship to shore at very short notice. So, as well as all of the technical paraphernalia and stores they also have their own support staff, particularly and most importantly a team of cooks and stewards. These unsung but hardworking men would be usually amalgamated into the host organization in the ship or establishment where the squadron was based. On board *Melbourne* the squadron stewards generally looked after the officers' accommodation and joined the team running the bar and serving the meals. But there was an additional duty and this entailed providing a duty cook and a steward running 'Wardroom 2'. Set within the complex of briefing rooms, locker rooms and squadron offices, it was here that the aircrew came to feed when their flying routines prevented them from using the wardroom itself at regular mealtimes.

The normal arrangements in such facilities led to them earning titles such as 'The Greasy Spoon' or the 'Trough'. The decor was often spartan with plastic-surfaced tables and tubular-framed chairs, the tables being decorated with grubby sauce bottles and salt containers incapable of dispensing salt. Plastic dishes contained margarine or butter and sliced loaves of bread still in their opened wrappers sat on the serving counters. An aroma of fried bacon mixed with cigarette smoke completed the picture. Sometimes a radio was belting out pop music from the galley side of the serving counter. But in *Melbourne* this was not the case. In *Melbourne's* 'Wardroom 2' at this time the quality of the food was exceptional.

Like most of my colleagues my night flying would consist of a two hour sortie, perhaps with another two-hour sortie after a break long enough to brief and have yet another mug of coffee in between. The routine I had grown used to in other ships would involve a take-off at, say, nine p.m. and so we would all troop into Wardroom 2 for a night-flying supper at about seven p.m. and tuck into the usual fare of variations on a theme of bacon sandwiches, beefburgers, chips, eggs, sausages and more chips. The smokers would start and finish the meal with a cigarette and the rest of us with coffee. Briefing for the sortie, often conducted as a 'self brief' would take place about an hour before take-off. All being well we would land back on the flight deck at around eleven p.m., sign the aircraft back in, spend five minutes discussing any defects which had occurred during the flight, descend to the locker room, divest ourselves of dinghies, Mae West life jackets and other trappings before returning to the briefing room to carry out a crew de-brief, write up any forms or reports necessary – a chore particularly applicable to the observers – and then arrive at about midnight in the Aircrew Refreshment Bar, otherwise 'Wardroom 2'.

This was where things in *Melbourne* had changed. Instead of the unappetizing fried stuff that I was expecting, we were regaled with such delicacies as smoked salmon, freshly carved cold meats, ham, fruit, cheese, sirloin steak and even plates of delicate little canapés. I began to look forward to night flying and wasted no time on return before nipping smartly down the passageway, my taste buds already anticipating the midnight gourmet feast.

A few nights later as I was tucking in to yet another range of delicacies I began to ponder on the circumstances leading to the riches set before us. I had noticed that it was only our squadron which seemed to benefit from the haut cuisine although that, I mused, was probably because we were the only squadron flying late at night. It was true that the Tracker boys did a bit of night flying but for the most part that was either early in the evening or early in the morning so they generally took their meals in the wardroom.

Like all good things, our high class catering eventually came to an end, and it did so in a rather dramatic style. It turned out that one or two of the younger and bolder squadron officers had come up with the scheme to improve our diet without – as they put it – anyone losing out. They had among their number a young and particularly small sub-lieutenant called Charlie. Charlie sported a light beard in an attempt to make him look a bit older and it was rumoured that he had purchased some built-up shoes during the previous visit to Singapore in order to, it was rather nastily said, enable him to see over the bar. My own principal recollection of Charlie was that whenever I climbed into a cockpit seat previously occupied by him I had to struggle to lower the seat from its uppermost position and fiddle about extending the harness straps before I could settle myself in the aircraft.

The catering cabal, as it came to be known, had worked out a plan centred on Charlie to assist the Captain and the Admiral in the disposal of their excess food supplies. They had discovered the existence of a dumb waiter which was used to pass food from the dry goods and refrigerated stores adjacent to the wardroom galley, up through a steel shaft passing through two decks to deliver supplies to the pantries serving the Admiral's and Captain's quarters.

All officers paid a daily messing supplement which was used to add a bit of flair and a few extras to the food provided through the standard ration allowance, such as a 'savoury' course after dinner. Senior officers such as the Captain and the Admiral paid a higher rate of daily messing supplement to which an entertainment allowance was added enabling them each to stock their pantries with all the goodies which were being coveted by the plotters a couple of decks below.

The cabal could work out pretty easily when the pantries were likely to be well stocked. Both senior officers had been providing hospitality and entertainment to legions of guests before leaving

77

Sydney and while operating in the Nowra area. Added to that was the fact that they both enjoyed the finer things in life, particularly in the food line and neither officer seemed to take much notice of how much stock he had in his fridge. Hence the cabal was presented with quite an attractive target.

The scam went rather like this. Although both Captain and Admiral were provided with comfortable suites of cabins in the after part of the ship they were each also provided with 'sea cabins' situated in the 'island' near the bridge and the operations room. When the ship was in an operational state or simulating this in an exercise the Captain and the Admiral tended to occupy the small sea cabins which meant that in such conditions the main senior officers' cabins were likely to be unoccupied other than by the senior officers' stewards, going about their duties during the day.

The plotters had conducted an experiment which demonstrated that Charlie, when folded into a semi-foetal position, could just be fitted into the senior officers' dumb waiter. The dumb waiter was operated by an endless cable which passed up and down through an inter-deck tube system and when it appeared likely that the pantries in the deck above would be well stocked, and the ship was quiet in the early hours of the morning, Charlie would be folded into the dumb waiter which would be then hauled to the top of its travel. Charlie would push open the folding double doors which provided access from the dumb waiter to the pantry, ease himself out and scout around for whatever could be removed without being too noticeable. The pantries were large with plenty of refrigerated and other storage space, so the pickings were fairly easy. Relatively small disappearances were unlikely to be noticed straight away if at all and losses could readily be justified in a busy catering operation where some form or other of entertainment was taking place on most days.

In fact, the system worked quite well for about two weeks as the force chugged north up the eastern coastline of Australia. Then we were joined by our accompanying submarine and the nocturnal anti-submarine exercises intensified, leading to an increase in the flying and more direct involvement from the senior officers. One night after a significantly more complex and demanding exercise involving almost the whole of both helicopter and Tracker squadrons, as well as the escorting frigates, the team slunk off to the lower dumb waiter outlet, folded Charlie into position and, after a few whispered instructions, hauled him laboriously upward. A soft call down the shaft told the haulers when to stop; Charlie hopped out and helped himself to a half used ham, a lump of beef suitable for steaks, a paper bag filled with savoury cheese tartlets, some apples and a hunk of yellow cheese. He piled some of this loot into the corners of the dumb waiter and struggled in with the rest clutched in his arms. At this point, the main door of the pantry was thrown open and a rotund figure appeared, silhouetted against the bright background light from the Admiral's day cabin. The great man groped for the light switch as Charlie tugged on the cable giving the emergency signal for hauling down. Nothing happened.

The fluorescent lights flickered on, revealing the stocky figure of the Admiral in a paisley dressing gown as the hapless Charlie cowered in the dumb waiter, clutching the incriminating booty to his chest. The Admiral broke the brief silence. "Who the hell are you?" he roared.

With great presence of mind Charlie shouted back, "Don't you know?"

"No!" yelled the Admiral, showing signs of rising blood pressure.

"Down!" screamed Charlie and instantly the dumb waiter dropped away through the shaft, the doors banging shut as it dropped.

The dumb waiter hit the bottom of the shaft with a thud and Charlie and the other conspirators were out, clutching the incriminating food, and running almost immediately. Two decks above, the Admiral was bellowing into a telephone, "Scruffy little runt running off with all my scran..."

A short distance away in his own cabin his Flag Lieutenant was holding the phone away from his ear and uttering the occasional "Yessir".

"And I want the scrungy little bastard caught and whipped around the fleet!" stormed the Admiral, as he banged the phone back onto its bulkhead mounted clip.

Thus began a three day search of the entire ship for Charlie. The remaining food was consumed, ditched or hidden, as was Charlie. Within an hour of tumbling out of the dumb waiter Charlie had shaved off his beard and disappeared into various hiding places in the depths of the ship. Next morning all of the squadron commanding officers were sent for and threatened by the Executive Commander, Commander Air and the CAG Commander in turn. Each of them denied any possibility that the thieves could be anything to do with their own squadrons and the C.O. of the Skyhawk Squadron was sufficiently miffed to point out somewhat forcefully that there were one thousand two hundred and fifty men in the ship and since the only identification was that the man was small with a beard, it could be anybody. It is possible that while offering this protest he was aware that typical fighter pilots were of small stature and several of his pilots sported beards.

Our own Boss, who had been enjoying the fine fare, must have had some strong suspicions as to the identity of the perpetrators but thankfully he kept them to himself. The late night suppers in 'Wardroom 2' reverted quickly to "anything with chips."

Chapter 7

More Sharks

As we travelled north, initially following the line of the Barrier Reef, occasional opportunities occurred to get in close at low level and see parts of this remarkable work of nature. At one point I took my aircraft down to about thirty feet, where we could actually see through the clear light blue water to the sea bed. Small islets were dotted about here and there, occasionally with some vegetation and with what looked like patches of light brown sand visible under the water between the islets.

As we flew slowly forward the whole area of light brown sand suddenly got up and swam away. What we had seen was not the sea bed but dozens – perhaps hundreds – of sharks all clustered together and moving very slowly, as a block, through the water. I was told these were leopard sharks but as we continued along the reef the same thing happened in other places and I could see from the markings and colour that there were many different species of sharks, part of a general population of many thousands.

Later on, in the latter part of the cruise as we were returning to Australian waters, passing down out of the Timor Sea and into the Torres Strait, I had been launched an hour before dawn to carry out a visual reconnaissance fifty miles ahead of the ship. As the pre-dawn sky grew lighter, I could see Cape York, the northern tip of

Australia, away to my right, but my attention was taken by a disturbance in the water initially about ten miles ahead of my aircraft. At first this gave the appearance of a bubbling blot on the otherwise smooth surface of the sea. The visibility was good with clear air and only a thin layer of patchy stratocumulus cloud which was becoming tinged with pink as the upper rim of the sun touched and then rose above the horizon in front of me. I was saved from the full direct brilliance of the sunrise because the sun was rising behind the patchy cloud. The cloud appeared much more solid around the horizon because of the effect of viewing it at an angle.

I had been flying at a height of five thousand feet but approaching closer to the curious object disturbing the water in front of me I allowed the aircraft to descend to two thousand feet and then, since I still couldn't make out what was causing the disturbance, I eased back the speed and dropped still further.

With about a mile to go I began to realise what I was looking at. At first it appeared to be some sort of battle taking place on and immediately beneath the surface. But as I continued the descent, with everyone in the aircraft trying to spot the phenomenon through the nearest window, the full picture of what lay beneath us was apparent. What we were looking at was the carcass of a cow or some other animal of similar size and shape. A pack of about twenty sharks were circling around, up, over and under the carcass. In their feeding frenzy, the sharks were taking bites out of their target and out of each other so that secondary battles were taking place with one or two of the huge fish setting upon another and tearing it to pieces.

The water around the immediate spot was a foaming, boiling maelstrom, with dark grey bodies shooting into the cauldron and emerging streaked with blood, indeed sometimes with blood freely running from their flanks. The dead animal in the centre of the mêlée was rolled and tumbled around and even out of the centre of activity so that the marauding sharks found themselves simply attacking each other in their blind fury as their real prey wobbled away alongside them.

I circled the spot for a further five minutes or so and watched as the carcass became smaller with chunks being torn away from it, but also now accompanied by a dozen or so dead or dying fish. The reddish brown stain of blood continued to spread away from the continuing but diminishing bubble of activity into the otherwise tranquil blue surface of the Torres Strait.

As we climbed away from the spot my own thoughts were drawn back to my brief but otherwise unremarkable encounter with 'Old Saucer Eyes' in Jervis Bay. In the intervening period I had almost forgotten the sense of menace, of dread that could be conjured up by the mere sight of one of these primitive monsters roaming freely in their own element, their own kingdom one might say.

The experience reminded me of the expression that nature is red in tooth and claw. I was yet to come across the 'claw' element but that early morning flight certainly demonstrated what the 'tooth' part could do.

We were all curiously quiet in the aircraft as we continued our dawn patrol without anything else occurring to disturb the development of a magnificent morning as the now blazing sun climbed further into the heaven.

Chapter 8

Hawaii

We sailed north, passing from the Coral Sea and leaving the wonders of the Great Barrier Reef far behind. With over 4500 miles to cover before reaching our next destination the small force of four escorts, the flag-ship aircraft carrier and supporting tanker had little time or fuel to spare and so serious exercising as well as flying was curtailed somewhat. This allowed the Admiral to send to the fleet a signal authorising a 'beer issue'.

The Australian Navy was nominally 'dry' when at sea. Alcohol was carried in all the entitled messes but none was served at sea unless the ship was sailing on passage, in a 'quiet state'. This rule was extended to other ships sailing in company and meant that if any ship was engaged in any moderately demanding activity such as refuelling from the tanker, transferring stores by jackstay, flying aircraft, carrying out an internal damage control exercise or a man overboard exercise, or even just launching a sea boat, then all the booze cupboards in all the ships must remain firmly shut. If the entire force was committed to a major exercise, the rule was applied to everybody even if nothing specific was going on.

In practice this meant that for most of the time when ships were at sea no alcohol could be consumed which could mean hundreds of men forcibly going on the wagon for a week, or even months at a time. It was generally and wisely reckoned by the Australian Navy Board that this would be setting a barrier too high for the average sailor so the system was modified to allow the senior officer present in a force to authorise a 'beer issue'. Things were still kept quite tight and when a beer issue was authorised it had to be done by signal and the signal had to specify the date, start time and completion time of each beer issue. No alcohol was to be sold, the signal said, before or after the stated start and finish times. It did not impose any limitation on when the alcohol could be consumed. In most instances the timing of a beer issue was after the end of the normal working day usually for a period of two hours. The Australians had not followed the Royal Navy tradition of the daily issue of a tot of rum for many years so the beer issue was just that. The sailors were each entitled to purchase two one-litre cans of beer providing the purchase was carried out during the period of an authorised beer issue. Generally the sailors who could, would take the cans to their messes for consumption at their leisure. One further precaution was taken to prevent hoarding – the cans were supposed to be opened as soon as they were purchased.

In the wardroom other arrangements had to be made. Dinner in the wardroom was normally served from 7 p.m. to about 8 p.m. and this timing usually clashed with the timing of the beer issue. It was therefore necessary to bring the meal forward an hour and send a discreet message around all the officers who could be reached to tell them of the new arrangements. The evening menu would also be changed to offer something simple and convenient to eat so that no drinking time was wasted. Steward service at dinner would be reduced so that maximum numbers of staff could be made available during the two hour period of the beer issue – and so the stewards would also have the opportunity to enjoy a drink. The manner of informing the officers of the revised arrangements was a simple note shoved under cabin doors with the inscription 'beer issue –

Scran at 6' or even, occasionally, 'bear issue – Scran at 6'. ('Scran' is 'Strine' (Australian) for 'food'.)

Every officer who could manage would assemble in the wardroom promptly at seven o'clock eagerly awaiting the opening of the bar and the start of the party. When the bar opened, the stewards, who had previously prepared a range of drinks, were lined up behind the bar exchanging drinks for hastily scribbled bar chits and in a remarkably short time the party was in full swing and the wardroom was packed with freshly showered and shaved officers, all clad in 'Red Sea Rig' – the informal evening uniform of white short-sleeved tropical shirt, black trousers with a black or brightly coloured 'Squadron' cummerbund connecting the two. Of course the bridge and engine room watchkeeping officers were absent but everybody else was there, glass in one hand and often a cigarette in the other.

At ten minutes to nine, stewards would begin to move among the revellers clutching 'chit' books and asking, "Last orders please gentlemen". The first time I attended a beer issue I was dumbfounded at the responses given to the stewards.

Typically, back came orders like "Four double whiskies please", "Three horse's necks" or "Five gins and a beer". As I gaped, trays of loaded glasses began to appear and amazingly they seemed to arrive alongside the proper customer without significant confusion or error. Within five minutes every flat surface in the room, with the exception of the bar counter, was covered with rows of glasses containing various spirit measures. Occasionally a taller glass appeared to be surveying the spirit glasses surrounding it. While I was waiting for confusion and chaos to climb into the ascendancy I spotted several officers digging deeply into their trouser pockets, emerging with what looked like multi-coloured miniature clothes pegs which they then attached to their own particular set of glasses. The wardroom began to look as if it had been decorated for Christmas, while the party continued happily along its way. The letter of the law had been observed – all of the alcohol had been purchased during the 'beer issue'.

I finished my 'last order' of one gin and tonic and stayed with the party for half an hour or so while my companions ploughed determinedly through their own 'last orders' and then, when I had decided to leave, I noticed several officers examining the tiny pegs clipped to the side of their glasses. I also noticed with some surprise that most of the glasses under examination seemed to have two or more pegs clipped to their rims. I moved over and peered closely at one of the glasses. The glass had two pegs. The first one was coloured blue, red and yellow with some tiny writing along the side of the peg. I looked closer. It read 'I have spat in this beer'. I looked over my companion's shoulder at the other peg which he now held in his hand. This one was all yellow and the inscription read 'So have I'.

****

The Fijian island group is situated roughly seven hundred and fifty miles to the north of New Zealand and about fifty miles from our direct track towards Hawaii. Some three years earlier I had been involved in a lengthy rescue operation after an inter-island ferry, the *Tui Lau*, had run aground on a reef in a rising storm. The rescue had lasted all day and afterwards the helicopter crew had been invited to one of the outer islands for a Cava Ceremony and the presentation of a Tabua, which means whale's tooth, the receipt of such a gift being regarded as a great honour. The whole thing had been quite an experience and the simple people of the island had been overwhelming in their kindness and generosity.

I was very keen to see the islands again so I talked the Senior Pilot into letting me lead a two aircraft open ocean navigation exercise towards the islands as the ship steamed close by the region.

The Wessex 31B didn't have any radar and the only electronic aid to navigation was Tacan which would provide a range and bearing to the master station, in this case located in the carrier, and providing the ship was where it claimed to be, the position of the aircraft could be plotted on an ocean navigation chart. This was all a bit cumbersome. As well as a possibly inaccurate ship's position being transmitted we also had to cope with anomalies which could distort the Tacan signal and reduce the already limited range of the transmission, not forgetting the necessary dependence on very accurate flying on a compass heading from the final Tacan position.

In the event, the Tacan worked reasonably well out to about thirty miles and then gave up entirely. Flying on a precise course for the next twenty minutes brought into view the first signs of the islands. Away ahead and slightly to starboard of our loose formation I could see piles of cumulus cloud in an otherwise fairly clear sky. I altered course towards them and checked that the other aircraft followed suit. Within another ten minutes dark smudges began to appear on the horizon. Climbing up to four thousand feet converted the smudges into the haphazard strings of islands that is Fiji.

Approaching closer, I descended to about five hundred feet, handed over control to the co-pilot and aimed my new super eight cine camera out through the front windscreen. We dropped even lower, skimmed along the reefs, over beaches and past hutted settlements where adults and children ran out to wave enthusiastically at the two Australian aircraft which had appeared from nowhere. At least two of the smaller islands appeared to have been privatised, with a big expensive house overlooking the lagoon from a high point, a smart motor yacht moored in the lagoon and very few traditional huts. We didn't get any friendly waves from this source.

We only had fuel for about ten minutes over the islands and all too quickly we had used up the time and had to turn back to the position where the ship should be but probably wasn't. At least I took with me some mental and some celluloid memories of the charming islands where with my colleagues we had been able to save over a hundred passengers and crew of that ill-fated ship, the *Tui Lau*.

****

The day seemed like something straight out of the musical *South Pacific*. The sea was blue and calm, under an azure sky flecked with tiny high-level clouds and criss-crossed with a few white vapour trails while the low coastline of the island of Oahu stretched away to left and right before us. Behind the shoreline we could see the jagged outline of the mountain peaks which dominated the centre of the island. The tallest of these was named Kamehameha, the name of the ancient kings of Hawaii.

The carrier had been spruced up nicely after the long ocean passage and she was now lined up for the approach to Pearl Harbor. Three Skyhawks formed a 'V' at the front of the flight deck, balanced by a single Tracker and a line of three Wessex helicopters further down the deck. The lines of sailors in smart white uniforms were set around the edge of the flight deck in what is known as 'Procedure Alpha' – the ceremonial procedure for entering harbour. Behind the stately aircraft carrier came the escorts, spaced at precise intervals, with the tanker and stores ship *HMAS Supply* bringing up the rear of the column. Aloft, brightly coloured flags streamed from the signal yardarms, spelling out *Melbourne's* call sign. I had joined a number of other squadron officers on the quarter deck and as we passed through the narrows to enter the huge harbour we could hear the explosions as a pair of saluting guns mounted on the flight deck above us began firing a twenty-one gun national salute.

We moved further up the harbour and boatswains' calls shrilled out salutes to the ships of the United States Pacific Fleet as we passed them on our starboard side. The order to face to port was given as more boatswains' calls shrilled the long single note of the 'still' in salute to the memorial mounted over the battleship *Arizona*, now a war grave for some fifteen hundred men killed when the Japanese attacked the harbour in December 1941.

Melbourne continued her steady progress into the depths of the massive natural harbour still followed by the four escorts maintaining their precise stations, with the larger *HMAS Supply* still at the end of the column. Of our accompanying submarine there was no sign. We were visiting Hawaii to take part in Exercise Rimpac 72 with units of the United States Pacific Fleet. These major international naval exercises usually conformed to a pattern. Ships from the participating nations would assemble at a major port of the host nation and several days would then be occupied by last minute planning as well as briefing sessions for all the units taking part. The ships of the various nations involved would then go to sea either in small groups or singly in order to carry out small scale specific exercises designed to work up individual weapon or sensor systems. The Pacific Fleet exercise areas around the Hawaiian Islands provided rich and multiple opportunities for this. As well as deep water anti-submarine exercise areas there were gunnery ranges where live firings could be conducted and a bombing range on a remote outer island complete with targets suitable to our Skyhawks. At the end of the period of individual exercises, the work-up phase, the ships would all be drawn together as a Task Force to spend about a week or ten days on the Operational Phase. This would entail pursuing a realistic wartime scenario where the Task Force would follow a route, possibly escorting a real or simulated convoy, while subject to attack from submarines, aircraft and a few 'Orange Force' surface warships. After this more demanding and hectic phase, everyone – or almost everyone – would return to Pearl Harbor for the exercise 'Washup'. This would consist of several conferences culminating in one grand conference when representatives of all concerned could argue about who sank whom, who did what and what should have been done instead. Record keepers and umpires would be on hand to guide the participants through the process of 'lessons learned' but inevitably these major international exercises would develop into mutual admiration societies in order to preserve the diplomatic niceties and international relationships.

The vast majority of the sailors who comprised the ship's company of *HMAS Melbourne* saw things rather differently. The international exercise was incidental to the opportunity to visit a romantic and far-away country where life was easy, the booze was cheap and plentiful and there were hordes of beautiful and willing women just longing to meet an Australian sailor. This latter factor was further emphasised by the Pearl Harbor tradition of greeting each visiting warship with a troupe of grass-skirted hula dancers weaving and willowing to the amplified sound of Hawaiian guitars. Unfortunately the image was rather dented as the great ship eased further along the jetty into the acoustic range of a United States Navy brass band belting out John Philip Sousa's favourites.

As soon as the ship was firmly secured alongside in her berth the formalities started. First to come on board was the Assistant Naval Attaché to the Australian Embassy in Washington. A tall slim commander in a dazzling white uniform enhanced by gold aiguillettes adorning his left shoulder came galloping up the brow, almost before it was even set in position. Thirty minutes later he was seen going back down the same brow preceded by *Melbourne's* Captain, also clad in dazzling white, before both of them disappeared into the back of a long black U.S. Navy car, to be taken first to the Headquarters of the Commander in Chief of the U.S. Pacific Fleet and then on a round of 'calls' traditionally required of the masters of visiting warships. A few minutes later the Admiral, rarely seen and not easily recognised by anyone outside the bridge and operations room crews, also toddled down the same brow, followed by his Chief of Staff and then by a young officer, presumably the Flag Lieutenant, burdened by no less than three briefcases. He too was wearing aiguillettes but they didn't look as shiny as the Assistant Naval Attaché.

A voice beside me addressing no one in particular intoned, "See that. They're goin' to apologise in advance, before the boys even get ashore."

While this was taking place activity around the ship had increased considerably. The band and the hula dancers had packed up and drifted away and the space alongside the ship was rapidly filling up with cars, vans and big trucks. Three brows now connected the ship with the shore and they were filled with officers, dockyard officials, customs officers, docks police, contractors and a motley collection of others. The two forward brows in particular began to look like 'ant highway'.

Chapter 9

Ernie has Another Run Ashore

Around me the quarterdeck goofers had begun to drift away. I looked at my watch and realised with a start that the morning was almost over. Like most of the squadron officers there would be little for me to do on board for the next few days other than attend one or two briefings and act as a hospitable host from time to time. Since we were now alongside, berthed in a dockyard, the 'beer issue' routine no longer prevailed and so, in the hope of a cool beer, some air conditioning and a chat with my friends I strolled off the quarterdeck, clattered down a ladder and made my way along the main passageway to the wardroom. The bar wouldn't be open for half an hour but although I hadn't seen any come on board, there was always the possibility of a mail delivery so I hurried along.

As I opened one of the double doors leading into the wardroom anteroom I was stopped by a wall of sound. The room was packed with people and although the air conditioning was going full blast it wasn't coping. Clearly the party had been going for some time and the stewards were already looking strained as they tried to cope with the continual demand, exacerbated in some cases by the unusual tastes of a few of the American guests.

I elbowed my way through the crowd, aiming to get myself a simple drink but before I reached the bar I was swept up into a mini party and included in a round of drinks being ordered. Everyone in the group was enjoying the experience of Harvey Wallbangers, some for the first time. The trouble with this simple mixture of orange juice and champagne is that it slips down quickly and easily, giving the impression of being merely a thirst quencher until, a little later, the alcohol suddenly kicks in. Shortly after that it can become a party stopper rather than a party starter as everyone feels the need of a chair followed by sleep.

Wardroom parties, particularly impromptu parties in foreign ports such as this one are well known for two 'indoor sports'. These were known both in the Royal Navy and the Royal Australian Navy as 'Baron Strangling' and 'Trapping'. Given appropriate circumstances and a modicum of luck they could be successfully combined into one activity. Looking around and listening to the snippets of conversation, most of which was being shouted because of the competing wall of sound, I gathered that 'Baron Strangling' was in full swing, and with a number of young and attractive U.S. Navy 'Waves' now being present, 'Trapping' was not far behind.

'Baron Strangling' is the art of meeting and entertaining people who have the means and perhaps the contacts to return the on board hospitality by launching into a programme of luxurious and grand shore-side entertainment that the original naval host would find to be well beyond his means. Americans seem to be inordinately susceptible to Baron Strangling. My own most successful Baron Strangling episode had also occurred on American soil – in Oregon. It was at the official cocktail party held soon after the arrival of a British ship in Portland, Oregon. I was one of only two helicopter pilots on board, and having shown one of the guests our highly polished and imposing Wessex helicopter my new companion stuck to me like a leech. Try as I might, I could not shake him off throughout the entire evening. I thought my evening had been wasted but next morning as I was having breakfast a note was delivered to me. It was a note to thank me and the ship's company for our hospitality the evening before. The note went on to say that a car had been left out on the jetty and I was invited to take it for the day "to see a bit of the Oregon country". I left the breakfast table swiftly but there was no sign of my benefactor. Instead there was a bright yellow Chevrolet Camaro convertible sports car. Inside on the seat was an envelope containing a special credit card to pay for any petrol required and a simple statement "Enjoy Oregon". I did. The wide open countryside and almost empty highways encouraged me to take the powerful little sports car up to near its exhilarating maximum speed – faster than I had ever driven before – or since. Fortunately for me there were no highway patrol cruisers out and about that day.

'Trapping' is the art of meeting young ladies for acquaintanceships which are not designed to go beyond the term of the port visit. Sometimes, if successful, undying love is declared, but for the most part such declarations soon fade from the memory. If the young lady is also wealthy or well connected, or is the owner of a car, 'Trapping' can be combined with 'Baron Strangling'.

Clearly the impromptu party in *Melbourne's* wardroom, already in full swing, had a long way to go. I looked around, cocooned by the roar of conversation overwhelming me, nodded politely from time to time while I sipped my drink deliberately slowly, simultaneously taking in the fervent activity in the close-packed knots of men and women filling the room. In the next group I could see, but not hear, Jim, the Squadron Operations Officer, holding court and enrapturing his audience with one of his 'outback stories'. To the best of my knowledge Jim had never been anywhere near the outback. Further over, Ernie was surrounded by a group of young American Ensigns. Apparently they were under training and had been brought over to see the antique Australian aircraft carrier and its elderly and strange aircraft. Ernie was in his element. He was a brilliant raconteur and had captivated his audience. Although they were young and unworldly, Ernie was giving a masterful performance of Baron Strangling. It occurred to me, that following his recent escapade before leaving Sydney, Ernie was in fact still under stoppage of leave – and bar, for that matter. A further surreptitious glance or two confirmed that Ernie was not paying for his own drinks or those of the guests, so he was not technically in breach of the bar restriction. All of the drinks were being included in the rounds being bought by Sam the Mirror Officer for the Tracker Squadron, the other Australian in the group. Unknown to me, Ernie was also alright on the leave front. This was because in the Australian Navy there was a rule – a sort of early 'Human Rights' rule I suppose – which declared that any officer or rating placed under stoppage of leave as a punishment, when serving in a seagoing ship, must be allowed ashore once during each subsequent port visit of more than five days. It transpired that Ernie was going to allow himself to be taken ashore that very night by his newfound friends.

Eventually, I managed to ease myself away from the party. I crossed the passageway into the wardroom itself and found a seat among the half dozen officers who were already starting lunch. The rest of the room was almost empty so after a quick light lunch I went back to my cabin and changed into clothing suitable for a stroll ashore.

This visit was my third to Hawaii, an experience very unusual for officers in the Royal Navy who tended to spend most of their time in the Far East shuttling between Singapore and Hong Kong with occasional forays to Thailand or Malaysia. I felt I knew my way around most of the island of Oahu but I wanted to explore a bit more in the north of the island, so I was going to try to hire a car for a day. I was able to fix this quickly in the Base Commissary and then I spent most of the rest of the afternoon wandering around the extensive Post Exchange (PX), a large and impressive shopping complex with attractively low prices provided exclusively for Service personnel and their families. Not for the first time I compared this with the NAAFI service provided at home. The NAAFI struggled hard to provide a similar service but didn't come anywhere near the slickly run government subsidised operation of the Americans. The NAAFI was of course better than what was provided for Australian servicemen, which was nothing at all. I made my purchases, walked back to the ship, picked up my long awaited mail, noting that all was well at the house in Nowra which was apparently enjoying the exacting security regime provided by a one-dog guard force. I started to write a reply but broke off to go to the wardroom and enjoy a quiet dinner.

Next morning all hell had broken loose. Ernie had been at it again.

Much as I had assumed, the impromptu wardroom party had developed and, egged on by the free flowing duty-free booze, Ernie's new friends had encouraged him to come ashore with them to see the town that evening. The party had broken up in the early afternoon and Ernie had taken advantage of a couple of hours to 'get his head down' in his cabin and thus regenerate himself for the evening's entertainment. He had sought out and found the Duty Lieutenant Commander, reaffirmed his entitlement to one run ashore during each extended port visit and sought permission from that officer to take his run ashore that evening. Unaware of the somewhat uninhibited party that had taken place during the afternoon, the Duty Lieutenant Commander had viewed the smart young officer in front of him, freshly showered and shaved, and showing no sign of any previous recent consumption of alcohol. The Duty Lieutenant Commander, who seemed to have no awareness of Ernie's former notoriety, had readily agreed. Before the conversation finished, Ernie was advised to be careful with strong drink, since, having been banned for a while, his constitution would not be ready for it. Especially, Ernie was advised, not to be led astray and to be careful of the local women. This fatherly chat, of course, and despite Ernie's composed, serious and thoughtful demeanour, went right over the top of his head, by-passing his brain completely. Ernie was totally focussed on taking up where the afternoon's party had left off, but in new and more exciting surroundings with new and more exciting people – of both sexes – to meet. He was raring to go.

An hour later, Ernie, still smartly but lightly attired, as befits the tropics, appeared at the after gangway, passed a pleasant remark or two to the Officer of the Watch, turned aft with a crisp salute to the quarterdeck before toddling off happily down the brow to the pier where a very impressive red convertible waited. Ernie whipped open the driver's door preparatory to climbing in before realising that it was a left-hand drive car, whereupon he tripped quickly round the other side and disappeared. The car prowled off along the jetty down the length of the ship before turning and disappearing into the dockyard complex.

The Pearl Harbor Naval complex is almost a state in itself. It has several airfields, the biggest being the Hickam Air Force Base, as well as United States Marine barracks and exercise areas. Ships are berthed and moored all over the place, often grouped by type but some of the most appropriate locations for big ships are now unusable because they are still occupied by the sunken wrecks of battleships and cruisers, victims of the Japanese Raid in December 1941. In addition to this the complex boasts a whole range of facilities for the servicemen, mostly provided or franchised by the PX organization. There were garages selling petrol and cars, shops, beauty salons, supermarkets, housing and – of course – clubs. These establishments were provided separately by rank and sometimes by trade. There were enlisted men's clubs, NCOs' clubs and officers' clubs. They each provided accommodation and all the facilities of a good hotel. They were comfortable, well run, fitted out to a very high standard and offered their services at modest rates. Above all they each had either one large bar or several smaller ones dispensing every kind of alcohol imaginable. On most evenings, particularly when visiting ships were in port, a Happy Hour was held. This was a period when drinks, already plentiful and cheap, were sold at half price. Happy Hours, which frequently lasted well beyond the designated hour, were designed to generate a party atmosphere and provide opportunities for otherwise disciplined men and women to let their hair down.

A little later that evening it was into such a roisterous mêlée that Ernie was conducted as he was ushered in to the Officers' Club in the destroyer berths. There were perhaps a dozen and a half other Australian officers present all being entertained by different groups of young Americans. In order to ease the food service problem and to avoid disruption to the flow of alcohol, the management of the club had laid on a comprehensive buffet which occupied one side of the bar room. The buffet was free and was intended to soak up some of the more awkward effects of the alcohol thus keeping the party manageable.

Ernie's new friends had planned to start at the 'Destroyer Club' to sample some local 'sundowners' – generously lethal cocktails of alcohol mixed with alcohol – before moving on out of the base to the downtown area behind Waikiki for dinner and then to while away the evening in one or more of the town's exotic nightclubs before driving back to the base and returning Ernie to his ship.

The evening didn't turn out like that. The drinkers mixed and mingled within the various groups. Long lost acquaintances were re-established. People grazed the buffet which was promptly replaced as it was depleted. Rounds of drinks were purchased and other rounds reciprocated. Music was introduced. The lights were lowered and dancing started at the back of the room. Ernie was in his element. By the time anyone remembered the original plan it was far too late to start a meal in a shore-side restaurant and in any case everyone had feasted to capacity. They stayed on and the night stayed young.

Through the now hazy view presented before him, Ernie sought desperately, if somewhat slowly, for a way to say thank you for the generosity, love and friendship shown to him by his new friends. What could he do to thank them? Another glass appeared beside him. Slowly, ever so slowly, he began to grasp the solution to his pressing need to offer something in return. He turned and pulled a chair towards him. Placing his glass carefully on the nearby table he climbed unsteadily onto the chair then, equally unsteadily on to the table, recovering his glass as he went. He was going to give them a poetry recital.

Somewhere along the line, nobody knew quite where, Ernie had acquired a classical education. He was also gifted with an exceptionally retentive memory which seemed to serve him well, drunk or sober.

As he stood up on the centre of the table, expansively opening his arms and causing a slight amount of liquid to slop from the glass in his right hand, several heads turned to look up at him.

Ernie boomed out above the throng the lines of Shakespeare's *Henry V:*

"Once more unto the breach, dear friends, once more; or close the wall up with our English dead! In peace there's nothing so becomes a man, as modesty stillness and humility:"

101

More faces turned towards the table-top performer, and the noise in the bar eased. Ernie ploughed on.

"But when the blast of war blows in our ears, then imitate the action of the tiger;"

He now had the attention of the whole room and, beginning to beat the time of the verse with his outstretched arms he continued, like a shorter, plumper version of Laurence Olivier. By the time he reached "Follow your spirit; and, upon this charge cry 'God for Harry! England and Saint George'!" the whole room was enraptured and several voices were heard echoing his final flourish "Yeah, for Hairy, England and *Saint* Geowge!"

"More, more!" cried the crowd.

Ernie launched into 'The Lady of Shallot' followed by Tennyson's 'Charge of the Light Brigade' but he had barely reached "Theirs not to make reply, Theirs not to reason why, Theirs but to do and die..." when he was hauled down from the table, back-slapped around the room and plied with more drinks from people he did not know and had not yet met. He was for the moment the heart and hero, the life and soul of the party.

Not to be outdone another would-be poet climbed onto the table to launch into some American poetry but faded as he reached the end of the second line. He was saved when another young officer broke into song. The songs took over for a while and, effort spent, Ernie slumped into a chair and surveyed his assorted drinks lined up on the table, so recently his rostrum. The party roared on around him.

Presently, Ernie dozed off into a booze-soaked sleep. As the party continued around him he slipped further down in his chair, now partly hidden by the row of glasses on the table. Gradually, as midnight came and went, others started to flop down into chairs. An hour later, Ernie was awoken by the call of nature. He wandered off towards the awful overhead sign proclaiming 'Little Boy's Room', located the gentlemen's lavatory and disappeared inside a cubicle. Having completed his task, he lowered the lavatory seat so he could sit and rest for a while. There, once again, he fell fast asleep.

The lavatories in this establishment were illuminated by a system designed to save energy, which switched on the lights in the room when anyone entered and was then detected by an infrared detector. The system would keep the lights on provided there was movement from the heat source – the human being in the room. Ernie slept happily on his uncomfortable throne for several hours. He slept through the declining hours of the party, through his new friends calling his name, through the noise of the staff closing the bar and, finally, through the call from the doorway into the darkened 'washroom' of "Anyone there? All clear?" And the slamming of the door.

Shortly after four o'clock in the following morning, Ernie awoke, dry mouthed, dizzy and befuddled. He stretched and removed himself from the cubicle. As he did so the whole room was flooded with light. Walking uncertainly over to the row of washbasins Ernie leaned forward and splashed layers of cold water over his face. Cupping his hands he drank some water and started to feel a little better. As his head began slowly to clear he stood erect, paused for a moment and headed for the doorway. He wandered out of the lavatory and through the connecting door to the bar room. He stopped in shock. Unaware of the time, he had expected the festivities to be continuing but the darkened empty room with disorganised tables covered in glasses spoke for itself. For the first time Ernie looked at his watch and was shocked again to see that it was nearly five o'clock.

The sleep had done him good and he was sobering rapidly. Although not sure quite which way to go he knew that he should head back to his ship as soon as possible. This club, being one of the smaller ones on the base, was a single-storey building with most of the space being allocated to the combined bar and restaurant. The bar itself occupied one end of the rectangular building, with doors leading to the kitchens and offices behind. The other end of the building was devoted to lavatories, a shower area and store rooms. Each of the long sides of the bar room was lined with large picture windows shaded by vertical blinds. On either side of the bar, double glass doors gave access to the outside world.

Ernie made straight for one of the exit doors. It didn't open and to his dismay he couldn't identify any means of opening it from the inside. Unfazed, he crossed in front of the bar to try the other doors, but with the same result. Clearly, he was stuck so he flopped down in a comfortable chair to consider his situation. He considered for five minutes and dozed for twenty. As he awoke he thought that it would be better to busy himself while he thought of some excuse for his failure to leave when the place closed. He got up and wandered around picking up glasses and ashtrays, carting them back to the bar. The entrance to the bar was not locked so he took the things he had recovered, piled them in one of the sinks behind the bar and began to wash them. As his head cleared further he started to enjoy his self-imposed task and, to help him make a better job of it, he switched on some of the lights. Two or three hundred yards away the sudden blaze of light caught the attention of a bored U.S. Navy shore patrol, sitting in their dark blue utility van with a wire mesh 'drunk's cage' in the back. The chief petty officer in charge nudged the driver beside him and said, "See that Will?"

As an answer, Will knocked the vehicle into gear and drove slowly towards the lights. They eased quietly to a stop and climbed equally quietly from the vehicle, the Chief easing the gun in its holster at his waist and the others hefting their night sticks. They need not have bothered with their stealthy approach. Their target was completely absorbed in his task and had made a pretty good job so far in returning the party-wrecked room to its former elegance. He was in the act of carrying four more highball glasses – two in each hand – back to the bar when a movement caught his eye. Turning to his right towards the point of attraction he was shocked for the third time that evening to find himself staring at two white-helmeted faces surmounting dark blue navy uniforms peering through the glass door at him. He dropped the glasses and overcome by unreasonable panic, hurled himself in the opposite direction, straight into and actually through the glass of one of the left-hand doors – and further, into the arms of the other two U.S. Navy patrolmen.

Ernie tried to explain, tried to talk his way out of the debacle but he tried in vain. "Name, Bud!" growled the Chief, leaning close to Ernie and breathing stale cigar smoke over him.

"Ah, Ernie," said Ernie before he caught the Chief's drift.

"Wise-ass, huh?" said the Chief. His henchmen crowded closer.

"No, no," spluttered Ernie. "My name is Ernie Nixon."

"You putting me on?" drawled the Chief.

"No, no. That's my name."

"You want I should whack him, Chief?" This, from the closest patrolman.

"Naw. We'll take him back and throw him in the can," responded the Chief.

Ernie tried once more. "I'm Australian!" he yelled.

"Nixon's an all-American name," said the Chief, suspiciously.

"But I'm Australian," said Ernie, this time more quietly.

"I think I should whack him – Now!" said the patrolman.

"What ship?" demanded the Chief. The other two patrolmen had now arrived.

"*Melbourne*," said Ernie.

One of the new arrivals said, "Hey that's the Aussie carrier that came in this morning."

"Ya don't say," said the Chief, slowly. Ernie nodded emphatically.

"ID," demanded the Chief. Ernie scrabbled in his pockets. As his hands emerged empty from each one a horrible vision was fixing itself in his frontal lobes, a recollection of an identity card, his identity card last seen lying on his bunk. Ernie looked crestfallen.

"Where's the ship?" demanded the Chief of no one in particular.

"Pier six."

"OK. We go to Pier Six – and if they don't know you there, it's the slammer for you, son."

The patrol shoved Ernie into the cage and climbed into the seats in front. The utility cruised off in the general direction of Pier Six.

Twenty minutes later, just before the routine morning 'call the hands' the blue U.S. Navy utility pulled up on the jetty opposite the after gangway where at the behest of the Midshipman of the Watch, the Quartermaster stepped out onto the brow and with unmistakable hand signals indicated that the vehicle should move up to the forward gangway. This was done not from any sense of protocol but because the forward gangway party was manned and equipped to deal with belligerent drunks and all the other problems that sailors in a foreign port were wont to bring back with them.

The truck crept forward alongside the ship until it arrived at the base of the forward gangway. The Chief Petty Officer stepped out, smoothed non-existent creases from his uniform and eased round to the back of the truck where Ernie was being helped out by one of the patrolmen. The ride in the truck and the night's revels had begun to leave their mark and it was a sorry-looking young officer who was escorted up the brow. The remaining two patrolmen stationed themselves on the jetty on either side of the gangway legs firmly apart, clutching their night sticks, emulating Horatio defending the bridge.

The question of identification then arose but since Ernie was a squadron officer and all of the gangway staff were Ship's Company no one was able to step forward to confirm Ernie's identity in the absence of his identity card. The ship's Master at Arms was summoned and appeared within moments. The Duty 817 Squadron Officer was summoned. The Officer of the Day was summoned, then our Squadron Commanding Officer and finally the Duty Lieutenant Commander. With each arrival Ernie stood looking more bereft and crestfallen. The Master at Arms, who was a good sort and well experienced in the ways of young officers, sought immediately to defuse the situation. He took the American Chief to one side and then invited him down to the Senior Chiefs' Mess "for a hot coffee". Seconds later a regulating petty officer appeared and wheeled away the Chief's sidekick.

The Squadron Duty Officer took a little longer to appear and was then sent away to see if he could locate the missing identity card. Within only a few minutes he was back clutching the errant card. This was minutely examined by everyone remaining and when they were all satisfied, Ernie was formally passed into the custody of the Squadron Duty Officer. They both disappeared back into the bowels of the ship as quickly as they could, and mercifully, just before the arrival of the Squadron C.O. the Senior Pilot and, inexplicably, the Squadron Senior Engineer Officer. Perhaps they believed it would take all three of them to hang Ernie from the yardarm.

Twenty-five minutes later the Master at Arms and his Regulating Petty Officer appeared with their guests and said fond farewells as they waved them off back down the gangway. Anyone moving close to them would have smelt the unmistakable odours of both coffee and rum.

Ernie was not the only member of *HMAS Melbourne's* crew to be returned to the ship in the hands of the shore authorities that night. There were many others. But he was the only officer.

Poor Ernie was back in the dog-house with a vengeance and that was sad. It was sad because he meant nobody any harm, he had caused nobody any harm, he had merely been carried away by his own enthusiasm and the circumstances of the moment. As far as the squadron was concerned he once again assumed the status of folk hero, the subject of embellished legend.

****

Later that morning some of us were treated to another little humorous incident. Jim, my friend the Squadron Operations Officer, had also been ashore on Ernie's fateful evening. He had returned onboard very late indeed, but being a much more experienced and well-travelled officer, he had avoided the pitfalls of excess hospitality and returned to the ship under his own steam. However, he didn't get to bed until the early hours and as a result overslept the next morning.

About ten past midday, I was sitting in my cabin, finishing off my letter home, and re-organising my pile of files and divisional papers when the door creaked open about eight inches and the familiar bearded face of my friend peered in. "What time is it?" he said.

"'Bout ten past twelve, Jim," I replied trying to avoid looking into his veined red eyes.

"Bloody hell!" he exploded and disappeared. Then things began to go awry. Jim had fixated on the fact that he still had certain parts of the Operation Order which he had promised to return to the Boss. The Boss, he knew, was attending an anti-submarine forces pre-exercise conference in the wardroom at 1300 hours that day, and so would need the documents still held by Jim. What Jim did not know was that the CAG Commander had invited the senior attendees from the other ships and authorities to pre-conference drinks in the wardroom. The event was well attended particularly by American officers who seemed to relish the opportunity to take a drink on board ship, probably because their own ships were strictly dry and not a drop of liquor was allowed.

When Jim had stuck his head around my door, from what I could see of him, he looked as if he had just fallen out of bed. His hair was tousled, his beard was unkempt and I could see that he was wearing an elderly looking vest over striped pyjama trousers. Jim had focussed entirely on the urgency of delivering the papers to his Boss, who, he thought, could be contacted much as I had been, by Jim simply shoving his head around the wardroom door.

Jim ducked back out of my cabin doorway and disappeared into his cabin. He quickly threw on a pair of tracksuit trousers over the top of his pyjamas, grabbed the folders and files, shot out of his cabin, out of our shared sprig corridor and into the main passageway which he trundled quickly along, while ignoring the surprised glances from the sailors he passed. In fact people pass up and down the passageways of warships in all manner of appearance and mostly go unremarked. What was unusual about Jim was that his strange dress contrasted with the bundle of official files he was holding – and he was heading for the wardroom.

As Jim arrived at the wardroom door his way was barred by a steward who said that the conference was about to take place. Jim elbowed the steward aside pointing out that he was not actually going in. Instead, he opened the door much as he had done in my cabin, only a little wider this time. Unabashed at the splendid array of uniforms, medal ribbons and aiguillettes assembled before him, he spotted the Boss in the middle of the room talking with a group of American officers.

"Pssst!" hissed Jim in what he believed to be a discreet stage whisper. Every eye on that side of the room, other than that of the Boss turned towards the door.

"Pssst!" hissed Jim, louder this time. Then, "Hey Boss"while he waved the clutch of papers through the partly opened doorway.

The door opened further, exposing more of Jim, which was unfortunate. The Boss, who had finally turned to see what everyone else was looking at, hastily put down his glass and ran to the door. He snatched the papers and snarled, "Go, just go." Jim was about to explain his circumstances but he saw the look on the Boss's face as the door was firmly shut on him.

Jim, who had a history of one or two scrapes in the past, was not unduly concerned by the incident and he loped happily back down the passageway to his cabin pleased that he had discharged his duty of handing over the necessary papers to the Boss. Thirty minutes later, a totally different Jim stuck his freshly showered and combed head around my door and asked if I fancied a run ashore that afternoon.

Chapter 10

Surfing

As we strolled towards the outskirts of the enormous Pearl Harbor complex in a warm subtropical breeze with the sun still high overhead we chatted about Jim's intervention to give the Boss his papers. Jim couldn't see that anything had gone wrong or could be considered inappropriate. He recognised that the Boss had seemed a little agitated but as far as Jim was concerned that was just life. "Things happen," he said.

"Well, they happen to you," I countered thinking of the story that he had once turned up for morning briefing in Nowra with a shattered egg on his head.

"Yeah," said Jim, "shit sticks," he concluded philosophically.

****

I hired a huge air conditioned Plymouth saloon for a ridiculously low price and with a few friends stashed inside we struck out along the Kamehameha Highway over the rugged central mountains of the same name towards the north of the island, where the real waves came in. Our original intention had been to drive around the perimeter of the island but about a third of it, in the north-west, was sealed off behind military wire fences so we had to make do with the unmilitarised remainder. Following the coastline around from the north side we came across a public beach called 'Pounders' apparently named after the style and size of the waves at that point. As we pulled up alongside a line of similar Plymouth saloons all apparently hired from the same source we saw that we were not the first to arrive at this beach. At least half of *Melbourne's* aircrew contingent was already present, mostly looking ready to challenge the impressive surf but some were standing on the fine yellow sand looking apprehensive. Unfortunately, although we were standing on one of the finest surfing beaches in the world, we didn't have one surfboard between us.

Body surfing was suggested and when the incoming waves seemed to become a little less aggressive I ventured tentatively into the shallows. I waded into the water up to mid thigh level only to see it being sucked away as quickly as I moved forward, leaving me exposed on fine wet shingle. I glanced down at the water retreating rapidly from my feet dragging little rivers of fine sand between my toes and I then looked up to see the front concave curve of a classic surfing wave not only advancing towards me but increasingly towering over me. Retreat seemed a good idea but there was no time. I could feel my feet being pulled forward by the shingle and then I was in a tunnel formed entirely by water. The giant wave curved completely above my head, leaving several feet of airspace between my head and the liquid ceiling above it. Seconds later I had been picked up by the wave and could see my new world rotating rapidly around me as I was turned end over end, time after time, being finally dumped on the sand and shingle slope where I had originally stood. As I crawled to my knees then nearly to my feet it all happened again, except this time I was dumped a little further up the beach. "The tide must be coming in," I told myself silently. But I decided to move a little further up from the jaws of the giant waves while I recovered my senses and my breathing. All along the beach I could see my shipmates enjoying – or sometimes not enjoying – similar experiences. Bodies were disappearing into the steeply curving waves and being flicked into the air, tumbled, rolled or turned end over end before being dumped like disused marionettes.

I went back to enjoy the experience of the waves for about another hour before collapsing exhausted to dry off in the late afternoon sun on the fine yellow sand which covered the upper half of the beach. Gradually all the would-be surfers trailed off the beach towards their waiting hire cars, most showing their battle scars of grazed elbows and knees from Pounders Beach.

We cruised down the eastern side of the island, passing the huge U.S. Marine base where I had enjoyed a barbecue of pig buried and roasted with hot stones on a previous visit, before entering the northern suburbs of Honolulu. On our way back to the ship we came upon the American Military Cemetery. This remarkable and moving site contains thousands upon thousands of graves, all laid out with military precision marked by horizontal headstones set into the lawns. The cemetery is set out in sections divided by roads and although it has many World War II graves it largely marks the shattered generation from the period of the Vietnam War.

We stopped at the cemetery for some while, which drove away the afternoon's former boisterous mood. As evening was coming on we motored in silence slowly through downtown Honolulu to return the hire car.

****

Back at the ship, the hot gossip centred around Ernie once more. When he had been delivered back to the ship there had been several instances of raised blood pressure, lurid oaths and broken pencils among the hierarchy. Ernie had been taken to his cabin and locked in, an officer guard being placed outside the door. This reaction had been dented somewhat when the ship's doctor, the 'Principal Medical Officer' had berated the onboard powers and informed them that Ernie must be fed, and must be allowed toilet and shower facilities. It had then been decided that breakfast should be delivered to his cabin from the wardroom. This proved impractical and having been heard being described as 'breakfast in bed' it produced more blood pressure and huffing and puffing, followed by the ridiculous charade of 'the prisoner' being escorted from his cabin to the wardroom where Ernie, now approaching hero status once more, was fed a gourmet breakfast while his guard, a friend from the squadron, tucked into a similar breakfast, his second for the day. Ernie was then taken back to his cabin and from there to the heads and the showers before being returned to the cabin. The guard took post outside the cabin where he had to shuffle back and forth to keep clear of the busy traffic along the passageway. Eventually he gave up and slipped into the cabin where he whiled away the rest of the day playing cards with Ernie, apart from a quick lunch break followed by a couple of illicit beers smuggled to the cabin.

Actually, Ernie had placed the top brass in something of a dilemma. One school of thought wanted him to be dismissed his ship or at least sent back to Australia in disgrace – having achieved the rare distinction of blotting his copybook twice. This of course would have cost a fortune in air fares, proved an embarrassment for our American hosts, cost the ship the loss of a pilot, and anyway, he had to be tried and found guilty first. Ernie was sent for, given yet another rocket, confined on board but not under close arrest and made to promise to be good. Ernie and his supporters of course thought he was just an unfortunate victim of circumstances and of humourless senior officers.

Chapter 11

To Work, and to Sea

All too soon our relaxation in the perfect Hawaiian climate came to an end. The great ship set sail for Exercise RIMPAC 72. There was no military band this time – and the troupe of Hula dancers was also conspicuously absent. Instead the jetty was speckled with cars of various type and hue, and alongside each one were one or two pretty girls, or a refined, mature lady, or in some cases, a veritable dragon, all waving, blowing kisses and calling earnestly to unseen suitors on the ship. The ship was once again arrayed in 'Procedure Alpha' for the ceremonial departure from Hawaii. Nevertheless some sailors assembled in their ranks were waving back, but, I thought, these were unlikely to be the targets addressed by the amorous acolytes on the dockside.

I was gazing down from my slightly screened position on the quarterdeck at the living manifestation of a combined and successful 'Trapping' and 'Baron Strangling' operation.

****

We passed slowly down past the naval airfield on Ford Island in line astern behind a bigger Essex class carrier and out through the narrow harbour entrance before turning to the west and winding up speed as we steamed towards our dedicated operating area. In the hangar the activity level had increased markedly as aircraft were prepared, trundled to the lift and then disappeared up towards the flight deck. The value of having a work-up period and starting it gently was demonstrated by a series of misunderstandings between the aircraft handlers and the maintenance crews when the wrong aircraft arrived on the flight deck and had to be promptly sent back down to the hangar again.

I was nominated as the planeguard crew that morning and so my aircraft was one of the first to appear on the flight deck. The rotor blades were spread quickly and efficiently, I completed my 'walk around' of the aircraft, fondling various bits of it and kicking the tyres before climbing up into the cockpit. I strapped in and as I ran quickly through the pre start checks I thought I could sense beyond the windscreen of the aircraft and the structure around 'Flyco' an atmosphere of angry impatience to get the helicopter into the air. Before I was able to press the start button for the engine I heard the flight deck broadcast booming out insults and imprecations to all and sundry to get the "bloody planeguard" airborne. My instinct had been right!

I gave the thumbs up signal, received the affirmative response and pressed the button. The engine compressor began to wind up, driven by the electric start trolley but nothing else happened. All of the other instruments confirmed that while important bits of the engine were whirling around it had not started. Suddenly there was a woosh and sheets of burning fuel shot out of both jet exhausts while the needle in the oil pressure gauge started a dance on its own. I drew my finger across my throat and closed the throttle, shutting the engine down. I wasn't inclined to try again until someone had looked at the failure of the start sequence – which was probably simply a failure of the igniters in the combustion chamber, producing the worrying sheets of flame – a phenomenon which was curiously called 'a wet start'. Nevertheless the prospect of being the only aircraft airborne and available did not encourage me to turn a blind eye to the defective start sequence.

As I walked unhappily away from the aircraft I took my 'bone dome' off just in time to catch the end of a trail of rudeness from the flight deck broadcast heaping criticism on my squadron, my aircraft and me. I was already pissed off and this unnecessary nonsense made me even more so. Throwing caution to the winds I spun round to face up towards the 'Flyco' window and with as dramatic a gesture as I could manage I threw my arm up in that direction with an unmistakable V-sign. Smiles appeared on the faces of several of the deck party surrounding my sick aircraft, preparing to return it whence it came.

The helicopter was folded, pushed onto the lift and taken down to the hangar. Within ten minutes I was climbing into its replacement. Interestingly there had been no summons to attend Flyco for a dressing and the subsequent broadcasts over the flight deck had been muted and confined to instructions to the flight deck crew. It was just as well because the attempt to use the flight deck broadcast to belittle me in public had angered me and I was more than ready to respond in forthright terms to any subsequent direct criticism. Actually nothing further was said.

I spent the next three hours hovering beside the ship, moving forward for the take-offs and dropping back for the landings, and occasionally popping back onboard for a quick suck of fuel. The Skyhawk Squadron went round and round, punching off aircraft after aircraft and following each other round for a series of 'touch and go' approaches to the deck. My boredom was only briefly broken by a Skyhawk launch where the aircraft was distinctly wobbly as it left the flight deck, staying low for a long time before climbing away. The same aircraft completed a circuit and approached for the first 'touch and go' landing and missed the deck completely. He came round again and was so badly placed for a landing that he received an early 'wave off' from the ship. This time, as he climbed away from his approach configuration, he banked sharply to port – towards me. As I responded by dropping lower and hauling the big helicopter away to the left, the shadow cast by the Skyhawk passed briefly through the cockpit. I heard the voice of the Skyhawk Senior Pilot come on to the radio and in soothing tones, attempt to calm down the young pilot in the errant jet. He guided the Skyhawk away from the ship for some twenty minutes while the other two jets airborne were recovered and quickly stowed down below, leaving a completely clear deck for the remaining Skyhawk. At last the small fighter-bomber was brought back to the ship. I alerted my crew to the possibility of a ditching or ejection while I personally mulled over the consequences to us of a crash on deck. In such a calamity we would not be able to land back on the carrier. Pearl Harbor lay a couple of hundred miles behind us and I was not sure where the nearest alternative deck might be – or even if there was an alternative.

The Skyhawk was lined up on approach to the ship, flaps and wheels were lowered and the pilot was brought down the glide path with the deliberate intention of breaking off the approach at two hundred feet and continuing on to overfly the ship. We watched from a fifty-foot hover, maintaining station a hundred yards to port of the round down. I turned the aircraft slightly to the right so I and the back-seat crew could see the approach of the Skyhawk. The black speck against the blue sky gradually formed itself into an aircraft, then into the familiar shape of a Skyhawk. The approach slope looked OK to me but, being to one side, I couldn't tell whether he was properly lined up with the slightly angled deck.

Nobody spoke in my aircraft as we all listened to the quiet calming voice coming over the radio, soothing and almost crooning at times as the Senior Pilot coaxed his young colleague closer and closer to the deck. Then everything seemed to happen at double speed. The Skyhawk loomed over the round down, floated briefly, then hit the deck with an impact which I thought must crush the undercarriage. A shout of "Bolter, bolter, bolter!" came over the radio and the Skyhawk's power came surging back on as the aircraft shot off the front end of the flight deck, staggered to just below the level of the deck and, as I shoved the nose of the helicopter down to race to the position where I believed the Skyhawk must hit the sea, I saw the little jet settle into a steady climb away in front of the ship. There were six arrester wires spread across the deck and his hook had missed the last one by perhaps a foot – no more.

The carrier turned away slightly to starboard, searching for a better wind over the deck and while the Skyhawk was away to the left of me on his downwind leg, the ship started to increase speed. The soothing, encouraging voice was still dominating the radio, coaxing, guiding, cajoling in a light conversational tone. I didn't really know the owner of the voice and I didn't know what sort of a pilot he might be but I recognised the exceptional job he was doing for that Skyhawk pilot. I also believed that this next attempt at landing would be the last because there would not be sufficient fuel for another.

Judging by my own airspeed indicator as I maintained station in the after planeguard slot the carrier was now doing its very best to get as much wind over the deck as it could so that the relative approach speed of the jet would be significantly reduced allowing the pilot a little more time to think and act at the end of his approach run. I estimated that the wind over the deck must now be over forty-five knots giving the approaching pilot the best chance he was ever likely to have to get back safely onto the deck.

121

The speck changed once again to an aircraft as the Skyhawk closed with the ship. Again I thought he was flying nicely down the slope and, if anything, was making a shallower approach than last time. Despite the efforts of the ship it all happened once again in a confusing rush but the landing spot was at least fifteen feet behind the previous spot and I saw the tail hook catch the second wire. To my horror I also saw the telltale change in the aircraft's attitude as the pilot attempted to shove the throttle forward again, believing he had missed the wires once again. The voice roared from the radio "Cut the bloody throttle." He did.

Almost immediately a different voice ordered, "Planeguard – Charlie, now." This was my instruction to return on board which I was pleased to do with alacrity.

Such is the life of a planeguard crew!

****

We ploughed on through the various basic flying exercises for the next few days until the Wessex Squadron was scheduled for a night time anti-submarine exercise, combined with the Tracker Squadron, and, joy of joy for the observers, we were to operate against a real submarine, *HMAS. Otago*, the Australian Oberon Class submarine that had accompanied us north from Sydney.

Both types of aircraft, the twin engine fixed-wing Trackers and the single engine Wessex helicopters were capable of locating and attacking submarines but the Oberon class of conventional submarines was particularly quiet and wily, so nothing could be taken for granted. The Trackers used radar for spotting submarine snorkels or periscopes with sonobuoys dropped into the water from the aircraft to detect the submarine by its underwater noise. The helicopters predominantly used dipping sonar, lowered well below the surface of the sea on a cable attached to the aircraft. When deployed against the same submarine in the same area, strict height separation needed to be enforced between the two types of aircraft to avoid a catastrophe. The helicopters flew around at one hundred and fifty feet except when hovering over their sonar cables which they did at forty feet. The Trackers flew above the area of interest at three hundred feet, generally in a race-track pattern. This all worked out very well unless, or perhaps more probably until, the helicopter experienced difficulty in maintaining a proper hover.

Most anti-submarine helicopters which operated by lowering a hydrophone detector or sonar set below the surface of the sea were fitted with a means of jettisoning the cable if they got into trouble. This would be achieved by the pilot pressing a red button in the cockpit which would fire a steel bolt through the sonar cable as it passed off the winch drum, thus cutting it clear of the aircraft. The Australian Wessex 31B was based upon the British Wessex Mark 3 but the Australians had replaced various pieces of equipment with equipment manufactured in Australia or in America. One of these items was the sonar set. The British dipping sonar carried sufficient cable to allow it to be lowered to about two hundred feet below the surface but the Australians believed this would be unsuitable to the waters they would need to operate in, so they took out the British set and replaced it with an American set which among other things carried enough cable to allow the sonar body to be lowered more than four hundred feet below the surface. But there was a penalty. In order to fit all this cable and the much bigger sonar set into the aircraft they had to turn the winch system around to face in the opposite direction. Unfortunately, in this position, the trajectory of the cable cutting bolt would enable it to pass through and cut the cable – just before it passed through the head of the observer. Since observers were expensive to train, the naval technocrats decided to remove the cutter bolts from the aircraft, neglecting the inconvenient fact that if hover positioning control was lost the only way to recover the aircraft was to attempt to fly the helicopter up vertically through at least four hundred feet before attempting to wind in the sonar cable. To give us some sort of chance these emergency manoeuvres were practised regularly but at night, with the adrenaline flowing and the knowledge of other aircraft prowling round just overhead, things could and did go wrong.

It was the middle of a dark and almost moonless night when things went wrong for me. The exercise had been running for about six hours and was due to conclude within another two hours. I had been airborne for an hour and we were maintaining good contact with the submarine target as we attempted to get into position for an attack. Already, my observer had carried out two vectored attacks using Trackers directed in to the position of the target to launch a simulated torpedo. We were doing well and had our tails up when for some reason known only to God, the aircraft lurched to one side followed by the auto-hover system overcorrecting and launching the aircraft even further to the opposite side. Ten seconds passed while I tried to recover the situation before the observer reported that he had lost contact with the target, presumably because the sonar body, some three hundred and fifty feet below the sea surface had been tilted over so that it was no longer 'looking' towards the submarine. The co-pilot said he could see the cable being dragged through the water as he looked out of his left hand window. "Raise the body," I ordered, as I struggled to maintain a 'wings-level' attitude, desperately trying to avoid moving backward or forward without any airspeed reference and also attempting to stop the helicopter being dragged down to hit the surface of the sea.

"Raise the body," was repeated over the intercom. "Cable's coming in," said the observer in a voice sounding markedly calmer than I felt.

"I'm flying it out," I said on the intercom for the benefit of anyone who wanted to listen.

The co-pilot followed this with "Four one seven – emergency climb-out, emergency climb-out" over the radio. The sonar body now seemed to be clear of the sea surface and I was able to move tentatively into slow forward flight although I still had no reliable reading on the airspeed indicator. As I did so I could feel the effect of the long cable swinging from side to side below the aircraft. "Cable's coming in slowly but OK," said the observer.

"Tracker nine – clear of your position, one seven."

"Tracker five – clear also." I was relieved. The threat of a mid air collision was removed.

"Cable's stopped. It's stuck," came from the back seat, this time in a different tone of voice.

"How much is still out?" I said over the intercom.

"About sixty feet."

"OK. Call the ship for me and tell them we're coming back, will you. We need a clear deck, low wind and enough light to see by."

I heard the message being passed on the UHF radio while I concentrated on flying the aircraft at a steady sixty knots.

"Tacan indicates Mother is forty degrees to starboard distance twenty miles," came from the co-pilot. I started to turn gingerly to starboard. These sonar bodies were designed with fins to maintain their upright stability under water but it was known that they flew badly in air and could oscillate wildly. I knew that it was possible for an expanding side to side oscillation to build up which could even threaten the main rotor blades, or if it changed direction the tail rotor could be at risk. If such a thing happened we would be history. Snuffed out in the time it took to drop into the water.

The aircraft was still turning slowly to starboard. I was glued to the flight instruments. I heard the co-pilot say, "Temperatures and pressures and all instruments are good. We have ten degrees to go. No sign of the body outside." The odd snatch from outside the aircraft had eased. "Stand by, stand by. Steady on that," said the co-pilot. I settled on the course indicated.

"Four one seven, we have you visual and on radar," came reassuringly over the radio. "You have nine miles to run. The deck is clear. Report your situation, over."

"We have sixty, I say again, sixty feet of cable outboard and unable to move. No other damage indicated so far." My observer was on the ball and thankfully making my job easier.

"Everything OK in the office. I can see the ship coming towards us," came from the co-pilot. I risked a quick glance away from the instruments and was relieved to see the familiar shape in front of us, lit up like a Christmas tree.

"She's turning to starboard – flying course, I think," from the co-pilot.

"Four one seven this is Mike Tango. You are cleared for a straight in approach. Flying course one two five. Deck clear. Lights on, over."

I took over the radio. "I see you Mike Tango. Dim the lights please. Approaching to establish a seventy-foot hover over the deck. Request height over deck guidance, over."

"Roger that, one seven."

I eased the speed carefully down through forty knots, transferring my gaze outside to take in the visual references available from the ship.

"You're high, one seven, down ten feet," crackled the radio.

Then, triumphantly, "Down three more feet one seven – we've got it in hand." A team of aircraft handlers had rushed out to grab the errant sonar body as it brushed the deck, starting to carry it away between them from beneath the descending aircraft, all the while being buffeted by the noise and downwash of air from above them.

The crisis was nearly over but we needed to get the helicopter down and clear before the Trackers and the other helicopter still on task needed to return. I eased the big helicopter lower, moving forward as I went, laying out the cable behind. As soon as the aircraft settled on its wheels I reached across to the central console and closed the throttle, then reached up and steadily applied the rotor brake.

Such is the life of anti-submarine helicopter crews.

****

Melbourne's Air Group had nearly completed the work-up phase of the exercise but among the few remaining requirements was the operation of the Skyhawk fighter-bombers in the strike, or Bomber, role.

As the more advanced Combined Anti-Submarine Exercises became fewer thus easing the demand for Tracker, helicopter and frigate time so the emphasis moved towards the jets. At the morning briefing one day the briefing room was filled not only with aircrew but was packed with all sorts of other worthies from among the ship's officers and senior ratings. Some I could recognise but others were strangers to me. The whole front row of the seating had been taken over, driving lesser mortals such as me further back and leaving even lesser mortals perched on the chart tables around the edge of the room or standing in doorways. We were soon let into the big secret:

"We have been given an exclusive allocation of the bombing range on X-ray Island," intoned the CAG Commander, in a manner that suggested the Almighty had just announced that as well as Manna from Heaven we were also to be showered with gold and incense – and it was all down to him. We 'Chopper Pukes' easily resisted the inclination to applaud. The beaming CAG Commander was replaced by the Skyhawk Squadron Commander, who now stood, feet apart, arms akimbo, dressed in his tight-fitting much badged lightweight flying suit ready to accept any additional accolades.

"We gotta take advantage of this so 807 will have priority over the briefing facility until after the raid – er – exercise."

A voice beside me said, "They didn't take any bloody priority when it needed cleaning."

"Fighter pilots," I said quietly. "Not allowed to get hands dirty."

"When you've quite finished," came ominously from the man facing us.

"As I was saying, this is a rare opportunity – I want to get every jet airborne and I want maximum input from every pilot." There was shuffling from the back of the room. The boys were not liking this at all. Nevertheless the towering figure in jungle green boomed on. I began to cogitate on how any man could stand up and drone on for so long without really saying anything at all.

We gathered that we were to become bystanders to the most important moments in the history of the Skyhawk Squadron – and we should recognise the privilege bestowed upon us. Before any of we, now temporarily redundant, chopper aviators could find a means of getting out of the room – to throw up some said afterwards – we were treated to a further series of explanatory briefings from practically everybody who was anybody in the ship. The Gunnery Officer explained the inner workings of five hundred pound bombs, then, not to be left out, his assistant chimed in with a dissertation on how big the bang would be. This particular chap, who didn't apparently have a name, seemed fixated on the phrase "And don't forget these are live weapons" which he inserted into his monologue every two or three sentences.

The Assistant Gunnery Officer was shoved off the stage, together with his large-scale diagrams of bombs and blast circles, by the Ship's Navigating Officer who told us where we were, then dried up. He was replaced by the Senior Met Officer who had absolutely nothing to say other than that at the moment he had nothing to say.

They droned on and on, and if the ship had owned a concert party I am sure they would also have been included. Meanwhile, singly and in twos, we lesser mortals seized opportunities to slip away and reassemble in small groups elsewhere to mutter darkly about "fuckin' stovies!"

What we had been introduced to was but the precursor of the next four days. Everything we had unwillingly heard on day one was repeated again and again in the following days. Fixed-wing flying came to a standstill while flying instructors, weapon instructors , engineers, analysts and the squadron hierarchy briefed their colleagues on everything they could think of. The few helicopter flights which took place started with muttered crew briefings held in odd corners and followed by delays in ranging and launching partly, we were sure, brought about by the absence of various key people from Flyco who were still enraptured by the never ending 'bomber show' in the briefing room.

At last the great day came. The ship was in position about sixty miles from the bombing range island. The entire ship's company were subjected to a long and unnecessarily detailed broadcast on what was to take place on this momentous day and the aircraft were brought up from the hangar festooned with a selection of two hundred and five hundred pound bombs. One by one the green-clad heroes of the hour trooped out to examine and sign the A700s – the aircraft technical log books – and then ambled across towards their respective aircraft, this time dripping with the paraphernalia of 'G' suits, oxygen tubes, life jackets, helmets and so forth. Each pilot was respectfully trailed by a small group of maintenance ratings who followed them around their aircraft before climbing up behind and helping the pilots to strap into the snug little cockpits.

One by one, engines were started and the jets taxied forward towards the catapult. A glance up towards Flyco and the port side of the Bridge took in the rows of anxious faces peering from every possible point. It was a big day for the 'goofers' and medals would probably be handed out on completion.

As each jet was positioned on the launch point, deck crew scrambled underneath to attach the catapult strops, while behind the aircraft a large chunk of the deck surface opened up to form the jet blast deflector. The ship was pounding along at near maximum speed with the bow pitching easily up and down through about fifteen feet under the influence of the long Pacific swell. The Flight Deck Officer struggled against the gale force wind whipping down the flight deck, leaning backward into the wind, green flag held aloft, eyes riveted on the pilot, waiting for the 'thumbs up' signal from the pilot. The jet's engine was then taken up to full power and, from the 'Howdah' protruding out of the deck to the left of the fighter bomber the catapult operator watched the Flight Deck Officer for the launch signal. The green flag then flashed down and the little aircraft hurtled down the deck in a cloud of smoke and steam to shoot out over the bows, dropping the launch strop before climbing away to join the others forming up to port of the ship.

As soon as the eight jets were airborne they fell away astern of the ship, the carrier's speed dropped and the wind over the deck, the eternal wind over the deck, eased sufficiently to enable conversation to take place while men were also once again able to stand upright. With a clatter and an additional whoosh of down draft the planeguard helicopter returned and flopped down onto its spot behind the 'island'. For a few moments everything seemed quiet as the 'goofers' emerged from their vantage points and other crewmen appeared on the deck and in the gun sponsons and boat platforms alongside.

The eight heavily loaded Skyhawks, now in neat formation as two echelons of four, swept in from astern. Flying at about two hundred feet, they passed down the port side of the ship and climbed away ahead, in the direction of their target.

"Stand down from flying stations." As the broadcast rattled out from speakers around the deck and in the hangar the deck crews strolled back to ready-rooms, the planeguard crew completed the necessary paper work and headed purposefully towards the by now almost empty briefing room, for coffee and cigarettes.

Barely had the coffee been poured when every broadcast speaker exploded into life. "Flying stations. Planeguard man up!" Men ran from every quarter, along passageways, up ladders, through the hangar and up to the flight deck. 'Goofers' were seen hurrying to reoccupy their carrion-like lookout perches.

Something had gone wrong. The jets were not due to return for an hour at least, but here they were, and, clearly visible, were all the bombs still hanging from their underwing mountings.

The planeguard helicopter rocked gently from wheel to wheel as the big main rotor blades wound up. Forty seconds later, lashings were removed and the helicopter lumbered into a hover over the deck, paused for a few seconds and then sheared away to starboard, to take up a position on the starboard beam of the carrier. Away to port the stream of returning Skyhawks were circling in a wide orbit at about five hundred feet. One by one they broke out of the orbit, turning away towards the empty sea area astern of the ship. At a distance of about six or seven miles, each bomb load was dropped into the sea. Huge splashes and some impressive explosions marked the drop point but it was obvious that not all of the bombs had detonated. Those that didn't explode sank in mercifully deep water, to sit quietly on the seabed twenty or thirty thousand feet below.

****

Now somewhat quieter, the Skyhawk pilots filed down to the briefing room, spreading themselves in seats around the room, awaiting the debrief from their Boss. An attempt to follow them into the room by the planeguard crew and a couple of other curious helicopter aviators was met with the door being shut firmly in their faces. Ten minutes or so passed before the large figure of the Skyhawk Boss strode, red-faced and head down, along the passageway and into the briefing room. The door slammed behind him and very soon afterwards loud and angry voices were heard coming from within the closed room.

Half an hour later a disconsolate bunch of jet jockeys wandered out of the briefing room and back towards their cabins. Little was seen or heard of the Skyhawk Squadron for the next few days and even when relaxing in the bar they seemed to lack some of their former zest for life.

What had happened was devastatingly simple. Despite all the preparations and bucket loads of expertise and enthusiasm thrown into the project from the entire ship's team of experts, one small error had crept into the plans at an early stage and no one had noticed. Everything was right – but the date scheduled for the 'raid' on the range was wrong. When the heavily armed squadron had shown up at the range and called for clearance on the range frequency they had been met with silence. They milled around waiting to enter the range and blow hundreds of tons of sand into the air while the Senior Pilot, who was leading the formation, trawled around the radio frequencies to try to discover why they were not being properly received. Eventually the devastating news came out that the range was shut that day, as it always was on that particular day of the week – every week!

It took quite a long time for our fixed-wing colleagues to live that down.

Chapter 12

Tragedy Strikes

We ploughed on through the tactical phase of RIMPAC and then returned to the waters just offshore from Pearl Harbor while teams were despatched ashore to attend various exercise conferences. These were divided between arguments over who did what, who should have done what and ensuring that only the good guys – the Blue Force – were deemed to have won the war. Other post-exercise meetings were devoted to the different nationalities pouring compliments, congratulations and flattery over each other. The whole panoply had been preceded by a multinational flag raising ceremony and so a flag lowering ceremony took place to mark the end of the exercise. All of the meetings were hosted by the U.S. Navy with hospitality provided in the form of rather good coffee.

While all the entertainment was going on ashore the ships of the exercise formed up into line and column and wandered about the ocean, just to show each other that they had not forgotten how to manoeuvre in company I suppose. Above the ships the various types of aircraft from the combined fleet formed up into international formations and flew about over the assembled fleet – again just to show they could do it.

Eventually the shore-side mutual back slapping came to an end and the Australian Squadron sailed away from Hawaii. The American participants hung about until we had disappeared and then, for the most part, shot into Pearl Harbor to let their hair down, tell each other what it was really like, recover the girls temporarily requisitioned by the Aussies and tell them tall stories of derring-do at sea.

As *Melbourne* sailed away towards the north, one of the last formation displays given by the Skyhawks ended in terrible and unnecessary tragedy. Six Skyhawks had launched to carry out a farewell flypast over the remainder of the American fleet, which resulted in several complimentary signals from our allies. When the aircraft returned to the ship to land on all went well until number five landed. The aircraft made a normal run down the glide path but was high on final approach. He banged down rather firmly, taking the last arrester wire and bursting a main wheel tyre in the process. The aircraft slewed to one side and, completing the drama, the oleo strut above the burst tyre collapsed, leaving the aircraft resting on one undamaged main undercarriage leg and the tip of one stubby wing. The deck was fouled and would take about twenty minutes to clear. This left the last aircraft of the formation unable to land on his home deck. The formation flight had been relatively short so number six had plenty of fuel in hand. He still had the opportunity of diverting to one of the American aircraft carriers or going in to Hickam Air Force Base in Honolulu. Instead it was decided that he should hold off in the vicinity of the ship while the deck was cleared. Flying in circles is boring so he requested permission from Flyco to carry out a few gentle aerobatics alongside the ship. This was agreed.

Robbie was one of the most amiable, pleasant, friendly and helpful people ever to be encountered in the then all-male environment of a major warship. He was a highly skilled fighter pilot and very experienced with the A4 Skyhawk. He was also one of the Fighter Squadron's Qualified Flying Instructors and had often been employed in guiding and mentoring newer pilots, particularly in the demanding challenges posed by deck operations at sea. He carried none of the grandness or pomposity that some successful aviators exhibited and he was as equally at home in the company of young sailors as he was with his peers or more senior officers. He had a profound sense of humour, was always game for a lark and was perhaps the most popular and well known member of the Carrier Air Group throughout the ship.

The 'goofers' were gathering in all the vantage points as the silver jet raced down the port side of the ship just above deck level and pulled up into a near vertical climb, rolling through 360 degrees as it climbed vertically. At the top of the climb it rolled over onto its back and gathered speed as it dived, inverted back towards the sea. Rolling into the upright position the aircraft pulled round to port in a steep turn before lining up once more with the ship's course. This time as it passed the flight deck it pulled up to execute a near perfect barrel roll.

The crippled aircraft by now had been moved from the deck to the lift on its way down to the hangar. "You are clear to begin your approach, six," came over the tower frequency.

"Roger that. One more pass?" came from the aircraft.

"Approved," returned Flyco. "You are cleared to join left-hand downwind on completion of your pass. Planeguard copy?"

"Planeguard copied. I'm remaining in low-level orbit on your starboard beam until cleared to resume planeguard station."

The little jet approached the ship from ahead, racing down the port side from forward to aft, pulling up once again, into a loop this time. The wings glinted in the sun as it climbed over the top of the loop, coming out into a forty degree dive towards the surface. The angle of dive began to ease, but too late. The aircraft struck the sea like a missile about two hundred feet astern of the carrier. The planeguard helicopter covered the distance from its station in a few seconds but the whole aircraft had disappeared beneath the surface of the sea. Nothing more was seen other than a few small pieces of detached wreckage.

The whole ship is plunged into gloom when a seagoing aviator dies in this way. His passing is marked by his colleagues who to the casual observer seem to be merely drowning their sorrows. But this is the way friends take their last farewell. They meet, talk of their lost comrade and drink toasts to his memory but the next day they will be called again to man their aircraft and do their duty. The death must be packaged away for later, and quieter, contemplation.

****

The ship stopped while boats were put into the water to search for wreckage but apart from a few tiny morsels of flotsam, nothing was found. A Board of Enquiry was convened and all sorts of technical and professional witnesses were questioned. Documents and logbooks were examined but nothing produced any reason why a skilled and experienced pilot should fly his aircraft into the sea on a clear, sunny, balmy morning. The members of the Board of Enquiry were unwilling to suggest pilot error as the cause and so their finding was that the reason for the crash could not be determined.

In the messes on board, conversations among sailors and officers dwelt on the record of *HMAS Melbourne*. Was there such a thing as an unlucky ship?

Flying was curtailed over the next few days while the ship steamed gently northward, heading for Yokosuka in Japan. Opportunities were taken to get ahead on the planned maintenance programmes for the other aircraft as well as to carry out essential checks on important deck gear such as the arrester system, the crash barrier and the catapult.

It was Sunday afternoon, the ship was quiet, with most of the ship's company taking the opportunity offered by 'Sunday Routine' whereby only work essential to the navigation and operation of the ship was taking place. I had nothing to do and after composing the bulk of a letter home I had decided to take some exercise and so wandered up to the Bridge deck. Out on the tiny port-side Bridge wing overlooking the flight deck I could see a group of about fifty men going through a rigorous bout of circuit training under the direction of one of the physical training instructors. Further over, on the boat platforms and other convenient spaces, groups of two or three were lying or sitting, reading and sunbathing.

On the forward part of the flight deck teams of flight deck engineers were working on the machinery. The jet blast deflector was being raised and lowered as adjustments were made and beside it the top of the 'howdah' could be seen, raised to its upper position about a foot above the level of the deck. Faces could be discerned peering through the glass from inside. Two men were working systematically along the catapult track, wreaths of steam curling up from the track behind them. The men stood back from the track while a white-overalled engineer signalled with his hand towards the 'howdah'. With a puff of steam the catapult shuttle shot up the track. Slowly it was towed back again down the track. The men moved in onto the track about halfway along its length and the whole process was repeated again and again. I looked away from the deck activity and peered around the horizon. I could see two ship-shaped blobs in the far distance, but nothing else. I glanced into the Bridge interior and back out again towards the deck. As I did so, I saw the shuttle hurtling down the track, trailing its wisp of steam. But the men were still on the track. Almost in slow motion it seemed, both were struck by the speeding shuttle. One was flung onto his back beside the track but the other was thrown high into the air, arms and legs flailing as he dropped back to the deck, lying still, across the track. All this seemed to happen in total silence because the inevitable wind across the deck together with the blanket of background ship noises drowned out any noise from the scene. I stood momentarily transfixed as alarm bells clanged from within the Bridge behind me.

Both men survived; one with nothing more than bruising but the other was a much more serious case with both legs broken as well as some cracked ribs.

I wondered again about the idea of an unlucky ship.

Chapter 13

Japan

The distant horizon lay under a thin blue-grey haze. This marked our destination – the port city of Yokosuka. I had never been to Japan before and I wasn't really sure what to expect. My impressions of the country owed much to World War II films and stories largely focussing on the appalling behaviour of many of the Japanese military, particularly in their treatment of prisoners of war. Shortly before leaving England I had been treated to an advanced private viewing of the soon to be released film *Tora! Tora! Tora!* covering the successful carrier-launched raid on Pearl Harbor which had crippled the United States Pacific Fleet and drawn America into the War. The film had been screened in a luxurious private cinema in Soho and after it ended the audience were entertained with a few glasses of wine and canapés while we discussed the merits of the film with our hosts. The producers had employed Lieutenant Commander Fuchida, the pilot who had led the raid, to help ensure that the events depicted in the film were authentic. I found myself being introduced to a small man, polite and unassuming and not at all like the caricature of the traditional Japanese we had all been fed in the post-War years. I remember asking Fuchida where the concept of the raid had come from. He had smiled expansively and his eyes twinkled as he replied, "From you of course." I looked puzzled until he added, "We simply copied the Royal Navy raid on the Italian fleet at Taranto."

'Of course, we had actually declared war first,' I thought but didn't say so.

Fuchida was a friendly, quiet and engaging man, so unlike the stereotype of the War and post-War years. I learnt from him that he had become a Christian and then a missionary after the war. He also gave me an insight into his friend Commander Genda, the tactical commander of the raid who flew in the aircraft piloted by Fuchida. Genda it seemed was a tough no-nonsense officer but very much the professional naval officer and naval aviator.

As the line of the horizon slowly formed into a low-lying land mass, lots of other impressions and questions whirled around in my head. I remembered listening to the raucous tales of 'runs ashore' in Japan immediately after the surrender, and the dropping of the two atomic bombs, told after dinner by the fat old engineer officer in my first ship – or rather the first ship where I had actually been allowed in the wardroom.

"You could get a run ashore with all the works on three bars of chocolate and a packet of fags," he was wont to say, followed by ever more lurid tales.

Only a few weeks previously I had read of a pair of Japanese soldiers who had just stumbled out of the Philippine jungle, dressed in rotting rags but still clutching their weapons and believing that the world was still at war.

The Japanese had moved from a post-War reputation where they had copied unashamedly every piece of Western technology they could find, to a position where they were beginning to innovate, outpace and lead the world in new technological advances particularly in electronics and car production.

The usual 'pipes' and broadcasts heralded the ship's company coming up on to the flight deck and lining the deck edge, now wearing unfamiliar blue uniforms, as we crossed Tokyo Bay and presented the ship ready for a ceremonial entry to Japan. Down aft, above the quarterdeck, the saluting guns began banging away to announce our presence as one who comes in peace.

"Secure from Harbour Stations." As the broadcast echoed throughout the ship, the officers and men fallen in around the flight deck and superstructure were dismissed and either drifted away or formed little groups watching the final manoeuvring of the ship alongside. As I walked across the flight deck behind the highly polished aircraft ranged on the deck for the ceremonial entry my eye was caught by what I thought to be an unusual cloud formation. I looked away and then back again, to see that what I had taken as a towering conical shaped cloud was in fact the snow-capped peak of a great mountain thrusting its head and shoulders through the layer of white cumulus clouds dominating the skyscape. I stood rooted to the spot for a few moments while I took in the sheer majesty of the perfectly formed mountain. I was seeing Mount Fuji for the first time and it was indeed a spectacular sight. I continued to stare at the mountain until the white cloud layer thickened sufficiently to hide the peak from my view. I understood there and then the magnetic effect that such a great feat of nature could have on people and how it could at once dominate and inspire them.

I drew myself away from contemplation of the mountain and made my way down to the quarterdeck to see what was going on there. On the jetty below me stood a dozen or so smartly uniformed Japanese naval officers with a selection of civilians ranging from dock workers to obvious officials and a few contractors. Behind them was a long row of vehicles headed by eight or nine shiny black limousines, followed by a selection of small trucks, single-decker buses and, in the distance a flock of brightly coloured taxis.

Along the edge of the dockside several gangs of dockyard riggers were easily and efficiently heaving in mooring lines and securing them to heavy duty bollards. In the water just behind the ship a couple of workmanlike little tugs fussed about looking for all the world as though they were frustrated at having nothing to do.

The dockyard workers continued their task of fastening the aircraft carrier firmly to the dockside. As soon as the mooring ropes were secured the gangways were craned into position and a tangle of power lines, telephone cables and hoses was carried into place. Teams of seamen attached the inboard ends of the gangways and almost immediately the various elements of the reception committee, led by an Australian captain bedecked with gleaming diplomatic aiguillettes – evidently the Australian Defence Attaché – began to stream up the after gangway. The Japanese officers came next, each welcomed by the shrill note of a boatswain's call as they were piped aboard, and then the collection of civilians followed.

Tiring of watching the gathering circus around the gangway, I made my way down to the wardroom which was crowded with our guests as well as ship's officers hoping for newly arrived mail and generally interested in what was going on. I was about to fetch myself a cup of coffee from the self-service tray on the end of the bar when I was pounced upon by the Executive Commander and introduced, along with a couple of other officers, to a group of Japanese officers. The introductions involved much bowing and handshaking and seemed to take a long time. Encouraged by the ship's Executive Officer we found ourselves leading our new friends out of the wardroom through the hangar and up towards the flight deck to begin a tour of the ship. This was evidently what they had come for and they made a great show of examining everything we showed them. My companion hosts were both Ship's Company officers, one an engineer and the other a supply officer so I took the lead in the tour of the flight deck. I had taken them through the mysteries of arrester wires and steam catapults when, as we strolled back towards the door into the 'island', they paused alongside the big crane, becoming immersed in animated conversation between themselves. As we stood patiently waiting, the tall Japanese captain, who I noticed sported aviator's wings on his chest, stepped away from the group and addressed me in impeccable accent-less English.

"They are comparing your ship with the aircraft carriers of the Imperial Japanese Navy," he explained. I nodded politely and assumed a look of informed interest as he continued. "They have noted all the advances in your ship but have noticed that it seems somewhat smaller than the Imperial Japanese carriers. However your ship is very efficient and impressive," he continued, "but of course the Japanese Self-Defence Force has no need of aircraft carriers." He smiled engagingly as he turned back to his group and, like a benign sheepdog, led them away from their debate and towards the bowels of the ship.

The tour continued through the engineering spaces and store rooms, canteen and dining rooms where, being a humble aviator, I took a back seat and let my companions lead the way. Much of this must have been excruciatingly boring for our guests but they showed absolutely no sign of being anything other than intensely interested and complimentary about everything they saw.

At last, as we completed the tour at the head of the after gangway, our guests having declined a further visit to the wardroom, they took their leave which involved a complex rigmarole of saluting, bowing and handshaking worthy of a Mack Sennett comedy. As the boatswain's calls trilled them on their way down the gangway to their smart cars I decided to go back to the wardroom for a drink and some late lunch.

I arrived in the wardroom anteroom to find the doorway almost blocked by a number of officers clustered around the notice board just inside the entrance. No mail had arrived yet but lists of events and visits had been pinned to the notice board each with space for officers to place their names. I saw that one of the visits on offer was a guided overnight climb of Mount Fuji followed by a session in a traditional Japanese bath house. I added my name.

It has long been a tradition in the Royal Navy and the Royal Australian Navy to hold a reception during the first night in port on foreign visits. A 'three-line whip' was imposed for all officers to attend the cocktail party so there would be limited opportunity for going ashore that night. The cocktail party was to take place in the hangar with the ship's band set up on the partially raised lift. All officers below the rank of Lieutenant Commander were assembled in the wardroom fifteen minutes before the scheduled start of the party for a pep talk. This included me so I went along to listen to a sort of advanced harangue, outlining the potential penalties involved in failing to act as perfect hosts. It was suggested with some forceful emphasis that examples of social crime would include monopolising the younger more attractive female guests, failing to ensure that all guests had plenty to eat and drink whilst keeping their own intake to a minimum and being drawn into offering political opinions. There was also to be an absolute ban on discussing the Second World War, or any other possibly contentious subject. I reckoned I knew how to behave at these events so most of the directives passed me by while I allowed my eyes to range around companions to observe their reactions. Clearly some of them were set on ignoring the 'advice' being offered and had every intention of heading straight for the women and the booze before aiming to finish the evening by achieving sufficient 'Baron Strangling' to ensure a subsequent satisfactory late night run ashore.

In the event, the party went as well as could be expected. The more effective hunters in the party appeared afterwards in the wardroom with either a young lady or a strangle-worthy 'Baron' in tow – or occasionally both! However they were soon gone to enjoy the delights of downtown Yokosuka, leaving the few of us remaining to consider the necessary preparations for the trip to Mount Fuji – to which we were now committed.

Chapter 14

Mount Fuji

The day of the trip to Mount Fuji started fine and clear. The aim was to complete the climb overnight so we could take in the spectacle of the rising sun from the summit of the mountain. This was the way it was done, we were told. We prepared ourselves with warm layers of clothing, strong footwear (frequently lightweight flying boots, I noticed) packed lunches in cardboard boxes issued from the wardroom galley and something to keep the rain out. It would take several hours to pass through the Fuji National Park and reach the start point for the climb so it was late morning when we climbed aboard the rather worn-looking bus supplied from the U.S. Navy base, complete with driver and two volunteer American guides to take us on our way.

We set off travelling ponderously through the heavy traffic of the city but progress began to improve when we passed through the residential suburbs filled with hundreds of neat small insubstantial-looking houses. The residential area gave way to open countryside full of small fields accommodating a few cattle or, more often, filled with cultivated vegetation of some sort.

The road started to rise gently away from the coastal plain and the land appeared more rugged and harsh. We were entering the Fuji National Park. The elderly U.S. Navy bus, which must have made many such taxing journeys, laboured and struggled as each hill became shorter and steeper while even on the downhill stretches the road wound and twisted so much that no opportunity was available to get up enough speed to tackle the next ascent.

We reached the stage whereby our ancient struggling carriage, having ground and graunched down through the gears, was reduced to walking pace as it reached the crest of each subsequent slope. Those passengers still awake were reduced to silence as they recognised the struggle of machinery versus nature they were reluctantly witnessing. Communal tension was eased in an audible and collective release of breath as the old bus shuddered over the top once more.

I watched the driver and the two guides seated together behind him. They did not seem unduly concerned at the reduced and laboured rate of progress so I took the reasonable view that therefore neither should I be concerned. That was the rational approach. Unfortunately as we advanced ever more slowly towards each challenging slope, the irrational side of my brain took over and I found myself holding my breath just like the others and even leaning forward, attempting to will the straining behemoth towards just one more effort. Then I happened to glance out of the window and catch a brief reflection of the road behind the bus. But I couldn't see the road. There was no road. Instead all I could see was a burgeoning cloud of dark blue smoke dense enough to hide a destroyer. I turned round and gazed, transfixed by the clear evidence of impending disaster following us along the road. I was still staring backwards when there was a loud mechanical clang, a wheezing noise then relative silence, broken only by the sound of tyres on tarmac as the engine stopped. I suspected that this was not the first time the driver had experienced such an event because of his very quick reaction in pulling the bus into the side of the road. The last of the slumbering passengers woke up. With commendable understatement one of the guides stood up and addressed the rest of the bus.

"We can take a break here guys," he said as though we had just arrived at a motorway service area. "We will be here for a little while," he added, more uncertainly.

Everybody clambered off the bus. We had stopped on the right-hand side of a steepish uphill slope with an even steeper pine-covered hillside stretching away up to the left and a low stone wall on the right of the bus guarding an almost vertical drop to a rugged looking valley several hundred feet below. The air temperature was decidedly cool and a crisp breeze was filtering down through the trees. After the noise inside the bus, the silence was noticeable. There was no sound other than the intermittent wind in the tops of the trees and the occasional crackle or gurgle emerging from the dying innards of the bus.

The engine cover in the back of the bus was lifted and the driver and guides gathered to mutter over what to do next. The driver had already made several unsuccessful attempts to restart the engine and now he had joined his companions peering unhopefully at the oily smelly heap of metal which had once plied its trade as a bus engine. The passengers were split into several groups. Some were sitting on the stone wall, oblivious of the drop behind them, while they ploughed through their packed meal boxes. Others had wandered along the road ahead to see what lurked around the bend and yet others were grouped around the guides and driver, listening intently and offering occasional morsels of advice.

Lofty, one of the Tracker pilots stepped away from the group, lit a cigarette and summed up the situation succinctly. "It's fucked," he said. No one seemed inclined to dispute this view so discussion moved on to what should be tried next. Nobody, not even the driver, seemed to know precisely where we were, or more to the point, where we might find the next bit of civilisation capable of accepting and passing on a message of our distress.

Plan A was formulated! The men who had scouted ahead up the road returned and reported that the slope levelled out just beyond the bend in the road and as far as they could tell, allowing for the continuing twists in the road, it followed a descent towards a valley which was at the same level as the land away below to our right. The solution, it was suggested, would be to gather as many men as we could behind the bus and push it up the remaining slope, re-boarding it at the top and coasting down towards what they were sure must be a village somewhere in the valley. Quite a lot of doubt was expressed over the likelihood of success for this plan but Australians are not easily put off by misfortune so we all gathered around the back of the bus and along the sides. Under the direction of one of the guides we produced a mighty communal heave – and the bus sat resolutely, unmoved. Taking the view that 'we were nearly there', and 'only a little more effort was required', the party assembled in their positions as before. This time the driver, having been indirectly accused of sabotaging the previous effort by leaving the brakes on, was instructed at the critical moment, mid heave, that is, to release the brakes. The bus immediately rolled backwards six inches before the brakes were once more clamped on.

Plan B was now considered. Three or four of the former scouting team were to accompany one of the guides along the road ahead until they encountered a suitable outpost of civilisation, whereby news of our predicament could be conveyed to the proper authorities. I thought we should climb back aboard the bus and settle down for the night, and maybe the next day as well. Others, less phlegmatic suggested we should demonstrate our feelings by gathering round the bus and rolling it over the retaining wall into the valley below before setting out to tramp back towards the ship.

An hour passed, then two, and having dozed for a while in the bus I climbed out to line up by the wall and pee into the void beyond when the noise of a motor vehicle made me turn to look down the road. As I did so, another U.S. Navy bus hove into view round the bend. My companions were already running into the road waving their arms at the bus which eased over and pulled in behind our tired old wreck.

It turned out that this bus was taking a party into the National Park but not with the intention of climbing the mountain. The second guide boarded what I now thought of as the rescue bus and they drove off following the direction of our search team. We resumed our wait.

After another hour and a half the U.S. Cavalry arrived. A small convoy headed by a much smarter looking bus – in army colours this time – was followed by a van with a repair crew, which was followed in turn by a huge breakdown truck. The first thing the repair crew did was for one of them to climb up into the driver's cab and turn the ignition key. The engine roared into life, but the vehicles behind disappeared into another massive billow of dark blue smoke. The engine was quickly switched off, the breakdown truck was manoeuvred into position and we all climbed into the replacement bus which drove away up the hill leaving the recovery crew presumably to find a convenient breaker's yard where they could lay the venerable old bus to rest. The road ahead did not follow the prediction of our search team, to descend steadily into the valley. It continued to twist and turn, climb and descend but on balance to climb more than descend. About twelve miles further on, we found the predicted civilisation. Our road team, who had been picked up by the first bus had raised the alarm and were now waiting patiently, sitting around a small café and bar.

With everyone re-joined we set off on the final leg towards Mount Fuji, which now loomed over us with every break in the clouds. Within an hour, we were disembarking at the foot of the mountain.

We had already reached a height of four thousand feet or so and in many minds the rest of the trip would be a bit of an anti-climax as we nipped up the mountain, jogged around the top and slid back down to a hearty breakfast.

It wasn't like that at all.

The last of the evening twilight was giving way to night as we set off up the slope. The mountain is actually a huge conical heap of ash and the well-trodden paths up the mountainside are also made of ash, in this case frequently beaten and crushed into a fine grey powder by the millions of feet which have tramped up and down. We quickly discovered several factors. The slope was much steeper than it looked at first and it seemed to become even steeper as we advanced up the mountain. The other discovery was that progress up the path was anything but straightforward. Every two steps upward resulted in slipping one step backward. The ash rose in clouds around our feet, penetrating everything and causing skin to feel gritty, uncomfortable and grubby. Whichever way we turned, the wind seemed to be in our faces and if it had been invigorating at first, it had quickly become chilly and was now downright cold.

As we first moved on to the mountain path I picked up some remarks, originally emanating from the guides, I presumed, to the effect that our climb was taking place just beyond the end of the official climbing season. I took little notice of this at the time but I was to have cause to recall it later that night.

We plodded on upward, with our group straggling out along the path, one guide at the front and the other making sure we didn't lose anyone at the back. After the first thousand feet a light drizzle began, which steadily became heavier. It combined with the ash dust already covering everyone to form a horrible grey slime. Everybody turned grey as we forged on through the darkening night.

Another thousand feet turned the drizzle into rain which had the advantage of washing off some of the grey muck but slowed progress even further. An aura of silence dominated the crocodile of unhappy aviators and such remarks as were heard were usually monosyllabic and mostly profane.

We continued up the forty-five degree slope and marched into the next problem. We had entered the cloud base which quickly formed around us as a thick fog. The whole group stopped while the more extreme stragglers were rounded up lest any of them wandered off the track or strayed onto the little side tracks which were beginning to appear. By the time we reached the seven thousand foot marker it had begun to snow. At first it was just occasional flurries interspersed with the persistent steady rain, then the rain gave way gradually to snow which quickly became continuous. At the eight thousand foot marker the group stopped again to gather into a more compact form and – a worrying development – our guides carefully counted us to make sure everyone was there. By this time I had decided that my decision to take up mountain climbing had been a rash mistake, but there was little I could do other than to continue to follow the leaders and plod steadily upward.

Another stop was called. The steady snow was lying on the path and the blizzard-like wind was forming small drifts around the edges of the track. We were informed that at nine thousand feet we would find a rest hut where we could shelter from the worst of the weather and since we were already beyond eight thousand we might as well continue on up to the hut.

The hut loomed out of the white maelstrom on schedule but when we crowded towards it we found that the only door was firmly locked. A notice on the door proclaimed something in Japanese and several other languages but curiously not English. A muttered conference determined that we had come so far that it would be wrong to turn back now, and somebody thought there would be another hut at ten thousand feet. I wondered if Mallory had thought like that on Everest before he was consumed by the mountain.

Since I had no alternative, I followed painfully upward with the silent mob. We trudged on through the deepening snow and increasing wind for probably another five hundred feet before one of the guides called a halt and declared, rather later than he should have done in my view, that conditions were too difficult to allow us to continue. "We must turn back," he said solemnly. I wondered how many silent cheers were joining my own.

The only advantage the descent offered was that the slippery nature of the snow-covered ash tended to increase our downward progress because every two steps down had another added to it as we slithered through the glutinous muck.

At first an air of depression hovered among the group but, as we descended further and conditions eased, the atmosphere lightened. "What the hell, we gave it our best shot and you can't do more," summed up the mood. By the time we dropped back out of the cloud and the rain had eased sufficiently to allow us to see the rough terrain spread out before and below us the mood had changed almost to one of euphoria. We were looking forward to the bath house and wondering openly about where and how we were going to get breakfast. Sadly we discovered that the packed meals already consumed were supposed to have included breakfast.

Back aboard the bus, we drove off down the road to the sizable village containing the bath house. The bath house was a large establishment which had developed into a successful business over the years based entirely on its steady flow of customers wishing to expunge the filth plastered all over them by the mountain – and of course on the convenient location of a strongly flowing hot spring.

We trailed wearily and hungrily off the bus and into the bath house where smiling young ladies dressed in colourful kimonos directed us to a long locker room where I assumed we were to deposit our outer clothing. The first member of our team to pass through the swinging doors into the steam of the bathing area wearing just a shirt and bathing trunks was shoved smartly back into the locker room. It dawned on us that we were to pass through the swing doors stark naked, first collecting a towel, soap, aluminium bowl and a tiny three-legged stool. Thus equipped we assembled on the other side of the doors where what was expected of us became apparent. The room was divided, as was the hot bath beyond, by an insubstantial hanging bamboo screen. We were expected to fill our aluminium bowl, squat on the stool and scrub ourselves thoroughly clean with the soap, rinse off by pouring the bowl of water over our heads and only then enter the communal bath. I set to following this ritual, noting as I did so that the first attempts to enter the water were being rejected by some large blokes clad in loincloths who were sending failed candidates back to do the cleaning properly. As I scrubbed away I became uncomfortably aware of a rising hubbub of female chatter and giggles emanating from behind the bamboo screen. The effect was altogether diminishing and rather like being the unwitting object of an audience assembled to watch a porn film. I made sure my preliminary scrubbing was as thorough as I could make it and chose my moment to head for the water, so that I arrived at the same time as several of my companions, keeping them between me and the loincloth-clad attendant. I made it into the water but very nearly leapt out again because it was so piping hot. I gritted my teeth, hoped that I was not being disfigured for life and submerged myself beneath the water. It took a few moments of acclimatisation but then the feeling of warmth and relaxation, contrasting with the horrible night on the mountain, became blissful. I lay back and relaxed. The only downside was the continuing twittering from the other side of the screen.

We stayed in the bath house for nearly an hour, hoping, I think, that the peeping giggling women would get out and go home first. They didn't.

By the time the replacement bus pulled away from the front of the bath house most of the pinkly glowing, newly scrubbed passengers were already lapsing into sleep. The journey back to the dockside in Yokosuka passed without further incident and we all trooped on board in time to devour the trays of sandwiches placed in the wardroom for tea – much to the irritation of the ship's duty officers for whom they were intended.

****

Two days later I found myself on another bus, civilian this time, which was headed towards the Mount Fuji National Park. This was an afternoon trip to see the natural hot springs and rugged terrain of the park, mostly to be viewed from the relative comfort of a cable car. The trip was a mere doddle in comparison to the stressful adventure on the slopes of Mount Fuji and I was able to relax, snap away with my camera and enjoy from above, the unique wilderness of the region.

On the way back, I joined several members of the group who had decided to be dropped off in a village outside Yokosuka, where we had been told we would find a community following the traditions of old Japan.

The bus set us down at the edge of the village. I wandered with two friends from the squadron down the principal street, which was lined with a mixture of tiny buildings housing a variety of businesses, mostly, it seemed, run by families. We spent a couple of hours wandering around the village, watching the residents clad in kimonos clumping down the cobbled street in sandals made from three pieces of wood as well as the colourful decorations found around the doorways of some of the shops. By this time most of the shops were closed and evening was rapidly coming on. The warm afternoon air had turned cool and we were beginning to feel hungry. We found an area at the lower end of the village which sported several small restaurants and a bar or two. The restaurants already seemed to be fairly busy and we moved from one to another trying to see beyond the decorative curtains and to work out what sort of food was on offer. Two of the restaurants, almost side by side, had similar displays in their windows. There was a card near the door which presumably listed the menu and prices on offer but it was all written in Japanese. The main part of the window was occupied by a series of garishly painted plastic models of dishes of food. It was not possible to work out exactly what they were but seafood and rice seemed predominant so we selected what we thought might be the best one for us and in we went. As we entered I could see immediately that we had entered the world of elegant, formal and traditional Japan. The establishment was carefully illuminated with suppressed but warm lighting. It was exquisitely decorated with pictures and plant arrangements redolent of a world gone by. We three paused in the doorway as everyone in the restaurant stopped what they were doing and turned to stare at us. I had been told somewhere that the Japanese considered it impolite to stare but clearly this particular piece of wisdom had not penetrated as far as the clients of this restaurant. As we stood there taking in the arrangements of very low tables with customers mostly perched on cushions a small delicately formed kimono-clad waitress glided towards us and with an elegant bow and a gesture of her hand indicated a Western-style table and chairs to the left of the door, behind the display window we had been viewing only a few minutes beforehand.

We sat ourselves around the table and menu cards were offered carefully to each of us. Our waitress bowed, smiled and waited. We studied the cards in silence. My mind flitted back briefly and irreverently to a Chinese restaurant much frequented by sailors in Union Street, Plymouth, where the standard order was "Big eats, John" with the occasional addition of "with an egg on it" which meant a lightly fried egg dolloped on top of a heap of rice and hot bits and pieces. I was confident that the fare we were about to experience would at least be very different to run ashore grub in Union Street.

The menu cards were arranged in two columns. On one side was a battery of Japanese characters and on the other what looked like a series of photographs of the plastic food models in the window. As we studied the menu cards without inspiration small glasses appeared on the table accompanied by a decanter of sake. I looked up to see another waitress, even smaller than the one tending to us but similarly clad. She bowed and backed away, keeping her eyes downcast.

Still patiently waiting for any sign of a decision and seeing that none was forthcoming our waitress very tentatively and carefully ventured a long slim finger towards my menu card. "Iss good," she said, "iss ver' good," moving her finger down to point at a second dish, and then "iss ver', ver' good," as the finger moved down to settle on a third dish. I smiled up at her and said, "We'll have that one," not knowing what I was choosing nor whether we could afford my choice.

Our charming waitress backed decorously away, turning when she had reached a polite distance, then gliding silently, she disappeared from the room through beaded curtains. The other diners stopped staring at us and returned to the dishes set before them. We turned to the sake glasses, raising them in a silent toast.

In a surprisingly short time the steaming dishes we had probably ordered, together with smaller plates of unrecognisable but tempting morsels were carried towards our table by the second waitress, followed and assisted by yet a third waitress. Little saucers containing sauces, chillies and other interesting things were added to the assembly. As we picked up the chopsticks to tackle the mixture of seafood, rice and vegetables, the principal waitress appeared and approached our table. She smiled, said something in Japanese which was probably the local version of Bon Appetit and then bowed deeply before backing noiselessly away and, once more, disappearing.

We concentrated on the dish set before us which consisted of delicately spiced lightly poached fish and shellfish on a bed of scented rice and accompanied by a crunchy salad. It was delicious and we each ploughed steadily through the meals in almost unbroken silence.

When the plates were empty and we had investigated the accompaniments in the saucers we sat there sipping the sake and feeling replete. I looked casually around the restaurant taking care not to concentrate too inquisitively on any other group of diners but I was diverted by the events on the big table dominating the far side of the room. A whole family was occupying about twelve places around the low table. Grandparents, parents, some other adults and four children of varying ages were sitting on cushions around the table, which was set with several big, heavily laden and colourful platters. As I watched something large and crustacean crawled drunkenly from the centre platter on to the table. As one, the family fell on it rapaciously, tore it to pieces and ate it. It struck me like a small horror story being enacted before my eyes. My companions followed my gaze with equally shocked expressions.

We decided it was time to leave and started the departure process by spreading a selection of local currency notes on the table and each separately attempting to catch the head waitress's eye. We need not have been concerned, she glided up to the table, bowed and then selected the required notes – which we were surprised to see did not amount to a great deal. She bowed again, and backed away to be replaced silently by waitress number two, who, in the style of what I imagined to be the Japanese Tea Ceremony – but probably wasn't – carefully poured tea into three small cups before also backing silently away.

We drank our tea while watching the family continue the process of attacking everything on their vast table and converting the careful presentations into wreckage. Our principal waitress appeared once again and bowed deeply before demonstrating that her vocabulary included at least one more word of English. "Taxi," she said smiling and indicating the door, beyond which we could now see the lights of a vehicle. We all stood, nodded to the waitress who bowed us out through the door to the local taxi which she had thoughtfully summoned. We settled comfortably in the cab and were whisked in silence back through the city to the jetty alongside the ship.

I was interested to note that the taxi fare seemed to cost us rather more than the three delightful dinners.

****

I had one more sightseeing trip while in Japan. This was to Tokyo by fast, efficient and crowded train. I was once again with two squadron friends and apart from peering at the outer walls of the Imperial Palace and watching immaculately presented and identically clad groups of schoolchildren doing the same, we didn't do much. Later when we got into the huge buzzing commercial centre we wandered around and watched as the curtain of heavy smog hovering above the buildings, waited to descend on the ant-like population below, scurrying hither and thither. We did decide to take a trip up in the lift to the top of the Tokyo Tower "built just like the Eiffel Tower in Paris, but taller, heavier and with stronger steel" or so we were repeatedly told. In the late afternoon, the view over the city would have been impressive if it were not for the fact that we were staring through the lowering smog which was already descending to take possession of the streets below. We took the lift back down and joined the tides of identically black-suited salary-men heading in full flood for the railway station. The journey back to Yokosuka was even more crowded and uncomfortable than the outward one.

****

The more experienced aircrew on board had carefully assessed and mapped out the various possible advantages attaching to each port to be visited. Hawaii offered high-quality sporting equipment at heavily discounted prices. This, during the first day in Pearl Harbor had resulted in a steady trail of aircrew back and forth between the main PX store and the ship, all lugging heavily laden golf bags, trolleys and other paraphernalia, labelled with the names of Arnold Palmer, Jack Nicklaus or some other golfing hero. In Manila, we were told, apart from the acres of massage parlours and girly bars, the things to look for were the markets selling rather competent oil paintings, watercolours and polished hardwood carvings. A visit to Tesoro's was also considered essential. Tesoro's was a huge shop at the far end of the main street, marked by a life-sized statue of a carved wooden Red Indian placed outside the main door, and where almost anything could be purchased provided it was made of wood.

Singapore offered several attractions. An evening visit to Bhugis Street to josh with the 'Kai Tais', the glamorous young transvestites who haunted the adjacent bars looking to pick up custom, followed by dinner around a table set up in the road at 'Fatty's' where the menu was offered as "You wan' fish or you want meat?" was an experience not to be forgotten. For some undiscerning individuals it was indeed an evening never to be forgotten, when, on sliding into bed with a lovely nubile and willing conquest, the horrific discovery was made later that the evening's companion was a 'he' not a 'she'.

For those who were unable to visit Hong Kong, and on this trip that included us, it would be important to visit the local tailors in Singapore. Shirts, suits, jackets and trousers were all made to measure very quickly but quality could vary dramatically so one had to be careful in selecting the tailor, which was usually done on personal recommendation. It was also de rigueur to replace the heavy and unattractive Navy-issue tropical uniform shirts and shorts with tailored drip dry versions but these were also readily available from the onboard Chinese tailor.

A 'rabbit run' to Change Alley to purchase Noritake crockery and cutlery, bolts of silk and watches was also important for the family men.

In Japan, it was said, the seriously clever aviator would set out to buy himself the biggest motorbike, tax and duty free, that he could afford and then, having first made suitable arrangements, stow the machine away on board, usually in the hangar. This was because Australian customs regulations allowed the importation of one motorbike per person free of all duties and taxes. There being no stipulation that the motorbike should be kept by the importer for a minimum period, the intention was that the importer would then immediately sell the bike 'as new' for an enormous profit, representing the tax and duty normally applicable to such a purchase made within Australia.

The theory behind this 'get rich quick' scheme was fine but in practice very few junior officers had sufficient capital to invest – it had to be cash – in the first place. Another obstacle was the lack of available space to store a big machine. Only two or three could be accepted on board and to get a space you had to be able to exercise quite a bit of influence.

One pilot from the Tracker squadron was much taken with the opportunity presented. Jerry was a newly promoted lieutenant commander in the United States Navy serving on exchange duty. He had the money to cover the deal and so, aided, abetted and guided by an assortment of self-appointed experts he set out to buy his motorbike. The fact that Jerry had never climbed aboard any kind of motorbike in his life was quickly dismissed as irrelevant.

The deal was done and the next day a huge 900cc Honda was delivered to the jetty alongside the ship.

Jerry was a really nice guy. He was very popular throughout the ship and nobody had a bad word to say against him, so quite a crowd assembled to see Jerry take possession of what quickly came to be regarded as his new toy. He and his friends prowled around the gleaming gold-painted machine as it stood on its stand. Inevitably it had to be started up and this was done quickly by another pilot who was used to riding big bikes around the dirt roads of New South Wales. The bike rumbled and purred as it sat upright on its stand. Having reached this stage it was but a tiny leap of logic that led to the need to ride it to make sure it would actually work. Since the bike belonged to Jerry there was no dispute that Jerry should be the first to ride it. Twenty minutes of earnest instruction ensued while at least three experts guided Jerry through the essentials of his first motorcycle ride. He climbed aboard and accompanied by a huge cheer from the onlookers, set off, somewhat hesitantly at first, along the jetty till he came level with the ship's huge overhanging bow, then he turned smoothly to the right, to return with increasing confidence to the start point. Having 'proved' the bike, it was wheeled to a spot beneath one of the small storing cranes and hoisted up onto the deck, where it waited until the lift could carry it down to the hangar. Here it should have stayed but Jerry could not resist the temptation to try the bike out again so it was hoisted ashore for a repeat performance on each of the next two evenings and again while the ship was alongside in Sembawang Naval Base, Singapore.

The bike did reach Australia without difficulty but then things began to go wrong.

Chapter 15

Fun with a Piano

While the rest of the squadron were wandering about Japan enjoying themselves, poor Ernie was stuck on board – or so we thought. In fact he had taken the opportunity offered by the programme of visits that had been arranged to show us Japan and which had drawn many of the senior officers away, to re-interpret the terms of his restraint on board. He was really required to stay within the confines of the ship but he had noted that the ship's standing orders included a statement to the effect that men under stoppage of leave who were required to work onshore within the dockyard or base area were allowed to proceed ashore in order to carry out such work but were required to report back to the duty regulating petty officer on return.

Ernie had initially volunteered to act as Squadron Duty Officer in order, he said, to allow others to enjoy the opportunity to see Japan. We still had a couple of aircraft ranged on deck so Ernie decided to check them regularly first from close up and then from the jetty. Officers of the Watch and the gangway crew got used to him coming and going, diligently strolling along beside the ship apparently examining the ship's side as he went. A couple of hundred yards ahead of the ship, there was a prominent square building which housed the U.S. Navy Officers' Club in one half and the Enlisted Men's Club in the other.

Ernie was smartly clad in uniform so when he went for his amble along the jetty it was clear to those on duty that he did not intend to go beyond the confines of the dockyard. On the first day he had just slipped into the Officers' Club to have a look around, and of course avoid all alcohol – other than a single beer that is. The next evening he stayed for two beers, met the manager and got on very well with him. Ernie had found a new friend.

The third evening of the visit was in fact the day Ernie had chosen to go ashore in conformity with the regulations which entitled men under stoppage of leave to go ashore once in each port. When the necessary request form appeared in front of the Executive Commander, duly endorsed by the Squadron Boss, it was at first rejected out of hand. The ramifications of Ernie's authorised spell of leave in Hawaii, including the embarrassing apology to the Americans for the damage to their glass doors, the cost of repairs and the totally undeserved tongue-lashing from the Admiral all left a rather raw wound in the Commander's psyche. Despite Ernie's clear entitlement, it took several attempts to intercede on Ernie's behalf before the snarling senior officer deigned to dash a squiggle on the much-handled request form. The Boss tried first, unsuccessfully, then, surprisingly, the CAG Commander and finally the Master at Arms whose simple logic won the day. "Well sir," he is reputed to have said, "it's like this, the officer is entitled to one run ashore by the regulations. If you deny it to him an' he cuts up rough about it you could be embarrassed."

"I won't sign it – get somebody else to do it," shot back the Commander.

"Sir," said the Master at Arms with as much patience as he could muster, "it says Executive Officer. If you don't do it, nobody else can. He don't go ashore. He gets pissed off. He complains and you get it in the neck – sir."

167

The chit was signed. Neither individual could have known that Ernie was not really bothered. He only wanted to go to the Officers' Club and he intended to go whether approved or not, just as he had done on the two previous evenings.

Ernie spent a convivial evening with his newfound friend and as the evening wore on he began to demonstrate another talent that none of us ever realised he had. He was quite a passable pianist. Beers came and went; Ernie played jazz, then popular classical pieces, then boogie and finally some ballads. He was an all-round hit and the club manager was delighted at the effect that his friend had on the takings at the bar. He also enjoyed basking in the indirect glory of being associated with such a clever entertainer. The evening went on long after the normal closing time and it was with something of a start that Ernie realised his Cinderella hour was approaching. With a final flourish around the ivories, toasts all round with the last beer followed by a Scotch whiskey chaser; Ernie legged it out of the club and set off along the jetty at a brisk pace with the cheers of his fans still ringing in his ears.

He had no difficulty in getting back on board because most of the duty staff were occupied by the stream of inebriated liberty men returning up the forward gangway. Many of them assumed on arrival that the gangway staff where all waiting to hear stories of spectacular runs ashore in Tokyo or Yokosuka. They were not, and a lot of effort was required to shift the happy wanderers away from the immediate vicinity of the gangway and off to their mess decks. Ernie simply took a deep breath, straightened his back and strolled up the after gangway, pausing at the top to salute the quarterdeck and acknowledge the salute of the gangway sentry before nonchalantly flipping his name on the officers' 'on board/ashore' board and disappearing into the bowels of the ship.

There were three more evenings before the ship was due to sail for the Philippines and with an expanding fan club Ernie felt he was committed at least to try and get ashore by reverting to the successful ploy already used. This meant he would have to go to the Officers' Club in uniform but this in itself would not raise any special interest because it was commonplace for American and some Japanese officers to drop in wearing uniform.

The evenings passed off much as the first two had done, except that Ernie added an additional refinement to his original procedure. He armed himself with a pocket-full of strong mints and decided to break off from his entertainment routine from time to time in order to disappear back along the jetty to the ship where he made sure he could be seen walking slowly along the edge of the jetty, casting the beam of his torch along the ship's side and pausing to examine the bollards holding the heavyweight mooring cables, the catamaran fenders and some patches of water. Since he was not a seaman officer, these objects were, of course, nothing to do with Ernie but to the casual observer it created an impression of diligent attention to mystic seamanlike matters outboard of the ship. To complete the picture, Ernie would gallop up the forward gangway having first ascertained from the jetty that there was nobody on duty at the head of the gangway who might recognise him. The mints were an additional precaution to prevent any sharp-nosed officer wondering why an officer who was so obviously carrying out some sort of harbour duty should have breath which smelled so strongly of beer.

In this way Ernie spent the next three evenings wallowing in the haven of the Officers' Club expanding his repertoire and circle of admirers in equal measure. On the first two of these evenings Ernie made certain that he was back on board well before midnight. On the third and final evening nobody knew when he actually returned on board.

Melbourne was due to sail at 0900 the next morning. A ceremonial departure was planned and so by 0800 the ship was thronged with officers and ratings – 'sailors' in the Australian lexicon, all dressed in smart blue uniforms. The two previously unemployed tugs arrived and lurked safely on the seaward side of the carrier. As the ship's company were lined up around the edge of the flight deck and in other prominent positions, two small trucks arrived on the jetty, stopping at each end of the ship and disgorging four or five dockyard riggers from each vehicle. The riggers split into twos and threes, taking up positions close to the bollards to which the remaining mooring wires and ropes were attached. The same previous selection of sleek black cars cruised into sight and various Japanese officers alighted to witness our departure. A Japanese naval band appeared from somewhere and began to play tunes which should have been familiar had they not benefited from some local rearrangement. However, the thought was there.

A blast on the steam whistle sounded from high up on the funnel, briefly blanking out all other sounds. A mobile crane with an impressively tall jib whisked away the last gangway and the main broadcast announced "Hands to Harbour Stations" which was thought to be a bit unnecessary since everyone was already at Harbour Stations. As the next broadcast boomed out over the ship and the surrounding dockside, a slightly built young officer clad in the white overalls beloved of the engineering branch burst into the Bridge. He stood clasping and unclasping his hands and demanded to speak to the Captain. At first he was shoved away but his earnest agitation was compelling and the Executive Commander demanded, somewhat brusquely, an explanation. Thirty seconds later the Commander shot out onto the Bridge wing, spoke briefly to the Captain and the departure of *HMAS Melbourne* from the city of Yokosuka was postponed.

The message brought by the Deputy Hangar Engineer was that a rather nice, and certainly rather valuable, concert grand piano had just been found in the hangar. This being an item not normally found in operational aircraft carriers it had been assumed that it did not belong to us – and therefore, by an amazing piece of deduction, it must belong to someone else and that 'someone else' might want their valuable property to be returned.

On the Bridge and in the other echelons of onboard power, the anger factor went up dramatically. Pencils were broken, fists clenched, accusations were thrown about and schedules for the departure and the rest of the day were hastily re-arranged. The rest of the ship's company thought it was a wonderful hoot and were collectively convulsed. Several rumour factories immediately started up and the fun began.

The dockyard riggers stood and stared up at the ship for a while and then sloped disconsolately off to their vehicles. The doors slammed and cigarette smoke curled out from the open windows to drift away on the gentle morning breeze. The Japanese senior officer farewell party looked at each other. The most senior officer turned and fired off a series of machine-gun like bursts of rapid Japanese and one or two of the others sidled towards the cars. One officer, on receipt of the instructions from his evidently none too happy boss headed rapidly off in the direction of the nearest building which happened to be the U.S. Navy Officers' Club.

On the Bridge of *Melbourne* a certain amount of confusion reigned. The ship's company were ordered to fall out from Harbour Stations and then, almost immediately were instructed to fall in again. The Second Officer of the Watch was reprimanded sharply for entering the departure delay in the ship's log and the reason for it. The Commander was not keen for this developing fiasco to be recorded and entered into the official history of the ship.

The two tugs meanwhile meandered happily up and down beside the ship. They were joined by another one which seemed to have arrived on the presumption that there must be a difficulty in easing the ship away from the dockside.

High up on the ship's 'island' superstructure, the Bridge wing suddenly became crowded with the Admiral, Captain and other officers, all staring down towards the flight deck lift which was just emerging from the hangar with a gleaming mahogany grand piano placed dead centre. The onlookers were temporarily shocked into silence, as a team of aircraft handlers gathered round the piano and began to push it towards the after end of the deck, clear of the 'island'. On shore the mobile crane was once more advancing on the ship with a long wooden gangway dangling below its jib. Shortly after placing the gangway carefully between the ship and shore, the crane with the tall jib still extended backed up and then repositioned itself alongside the after end of the flight deck. As it did so a flatbed lorry with U.S. markings arrived and stopped a few yards down from the crane.

The Executive Commander went trotting down the ladders and stairways to the starboard main deck where the returned gangway was just being placed in position. He was followed by the CAG Commander and a midshipman as he climbed onto the slightly rocking gangway and marched smartly down along it and across to the Japanese admiral. He saluted briskly and was discomforted to receive both a salute and a deep bow in return. He could then be seen talking earnestly to the senior officer, waving his hands about by way of explanation as the latter stood ramrod straight, hands by his sides, listening carefully. Some of the other Japanese officers moved closer. By the time the Commander had finished his apology and was trying to combine a bow with a naval salute the aircraft handlers had completed the necessary task of swathing the piano in blankets and cardboard and the team leader was standing beside his handiwork looking expectantly at the crane. The crane trundled a few feet forward then extended and planted its hydraulic 'feet' down on to the tarmac as the jib stretched itself to loom over the flight deck. The men on the deck reached out, took the two canvass strops dangling from the crane hook and delicately fitted them around the piano. The crane took the strain and the piano began to rise from the deck. At a height of about eight feet above the deck the whole package listed rapidly sideways. It was quickly lowered back to the deck while strops were repositioned and packaging checked. The crane took the strain again and this time the piano lurched even more quickly the other way. Engineers now appeared to examine the security of the load and once more the whole team stood back in silence while the crane inched its precious load off the deck. This time it worked. The jib was trained slowly around to plumb the back of the lorry before the piano was lowered equally carefully down to the guiding hands of several men clustered on the back of the vehicle.

The ship cast off the remaining lines at 1100, two hours later than planned. The ship's company were stood down from the ceremonial departure procedure. The aircraft ranged on deck were pushed onto the lift and taken down to the hangar, with the exception of the planeguard helicopter. The ship moved slowly across the harbour, preceded by one tug and followed by the other. The third tug had swallowed his curiosity and disappeared off to some other part of the harbour. As the remaining two tugs sheered off the inquiry into the incident of the stowaway piano led by the Master at Arms had already begun. The Admiral, a man who had obviously missed the queue when God had issued senses of humour, was said to be in a filthy uncompromising mood and deemed unapproachable. The Captain wasn't much better, demanding "heads must roll" at every opportunity. The Air Group had been planning a full day of basic work-up training which was now being hastily reorganised.

Signals flashed back and forth to the Japanese and American shore authorities apologising and demanding information in equal measure. At first all the eyes of authority turned towards Ernie but since he was confined on board apart from one day in the middle of the visit he seemed untouchable. Nevertheless, suspicions remained and senior officers were encountered muttering in huddles from time to time.

Ernie went about his business without any interest in the events of the morning. He was tackled at one stage by the Captain's Secretary, an unpopular man mistrusted by the aircrew. "You were responsible for that piano," he said, glaring through thick-lensed glasses directly into Ernie's eyes.

"What piano was that, sir?" came back the innocent reply.

"We'll soon find out from shore." The Captain's Secretary stalked off. Ernie retained his air of innocence and kept well clear of the subject of musical instruments of any kind. In fact, Ernie had taken precautions. On the recent evenings when he had entered the Officers' Club he had quickly replaced his uniform jacket with a lightweight civilian coat. He had worn tinted glasses and had never used his proper name. He had also kept the fact that he was an aviator to himself.

As the truncated work-up wore on through the day everyone found other things to think about and the piano incident dropped, at least temporarily out of sight and out of mind. The signals received from shore had been universally unhelpful in the matter of the piano. There were several assertions that the piano had been in its usual place when the club had finally closed on the night before sailing. No one could account for the fact that a lorry, a crane and a skilled crane driver would have been required to move the piano out of the club and into the hangar of *Melbourne*. And anyway, it was said, how could it be that none of the duty personnel on board the carrier noticed the arrival of a large shiny grand piano – and how did it make its way unseen down into the hangar?

The day flying programme came to an end without incident and the ship settled down to passage routine. There was to be no night flying so everyone relaxed and emerged, freshly showered, into the wardroom anteroom in the hope that a 'beer issue' would be announced. At eight o'clock when most officers were at dinner, it was. Meals were quickly concluded and everyone moved towards the bar. The next hour and a half were convivial but the usual scramble to pack in as many drinks as possible in the time available did not occur so at a little before ten, the bar area of the anteroom was fairly sparsely populated when no less than six commanders, led by the Executive Commander entered the mess and, talking among themselves as to whether to finish the evening with a large port or Madeira they assembled around the bar, which was now surrounded by six chrome, leather and cane bar stools of obvious style and quality. Led by the Executive Commander they each climbed up onto a stool and settled back to await the arrival of their post-dinner drinks. All the stools had been empty as the group entered the room and, led by the Executive Commander they had walked straight to the stools, almost as though taking places deliberately left for them. "These are very nice," said the doctor, picking up his glass of port.

"Yeah, very comfortable," added the small plump Engineer Commander, working his way more firmly into the bucket seat on the top of his stool while his legs dangled and searched for the supporting chromium rung. The conversation, such as it was, died away as glasses were raised.

"They came with the piano," said the barman helpfully. The Executive Commander's arm stopped abruptly with his glass raised halfway to his lips and the colour drained from his face. The others followed suit and suddenly, as though a charge of electricity had been passed through the stools, they all leapt off. The Engineer Commander was the last to stand behind the offending stools as the six senior officers stood staring in horror at was about to become the cause of even more drama and acrimony.

Later that night, after more harsh words had been heard passing around among the hierarchy, one of the twin engine anti-submarine Trackers was ranged on deck, while the crew consisting of just the two pilots, were down below briefing for a special mission. Just after midnight the aircraft roared into the mercifully benign moonlit sky, with the tactical operator's rear cabin filled with two rather smart cane, leather and chrome bar stools placed across the seats. Just over an hour later, the aircraft returned to land on, collect two more stools and launch from the catapult only ten minutes later. It was nearly 5 a.m. and the first light of dawn was colouring the sky before the aircraft returned from the third trip ashore and the ship was finally able to stand down from flying stations.

It was said that the 'Godfathers' were unapproachable in their fury.

Chapter 16

Manila

We steamed steadily south and the 'great piano enquiry' rumbled on ineffectively throughout the ship. Blame for the embarrassment was sloshed around in bucket-fulls and acrimony was the order of the day particularly among the senior brass and the more seriously disposed 'fish-heads' (non-aviating seaman branch personnel). Within the squadrons the incidents of the piano and bar stools was an intriguing and amusing source of gossip and innuendo. Ernie remained a major suspect but he had a cast-iron alibi. In response to the repeated attempts to get him to admit involvement he merely shrugged, giving the impression that not only did he not know what was being spoken of but additionally that the subject was of absolutely no interest or concern to him.

The ship needed to catch up on the time lost by waiting about while the bar stools were flown ashore so the flying programme had been curtailed even more than previously decided, which allowed the maintenance crews to catch up on planned maintenance programmes. This was useful because it meant that the aircraft would be well prepared for the extensive flying expected after departure from the Philippines. We were to spend about ten days or so carrying out tactical exercises with units of the U.S. Navy from the giant United States base at Subic Bay, close to Manila where we were to be berthed.

Ten days after leaving Japan we eased around to the south of the long central breakwater guarding the entrance to the wide expanse of Manila Harbor. Once again the ship was carrying out a ceremonial entry to the harbour with a selection of cleaned and polished aircraft ranged on deck and the ship's company lining the deck edge. We were back in white tropical uniforms which seemed to make everyone more comfortable. As we slowly approached our alongside berth we were able to peer up through the blue dome above us but a grubby haze intervened between the ship and the harbour-side buildings. It was said that the enormous sprawl of the city of Manila could produce its own weather system and I could well understand that. We trundled in through the dispersing smog, eventually easing alongside an otherwise empty pier. The reception committee assembled onshore was noticeably smaller than at Yokosuka and there was no visit programme such as we had enjoyed in Japan. We were expected to make our own entertainment when going ashore and the ship's company were more than happy with that arrangement. The Philippines could be a wild and unforgiving place in the early nineteen seventies. Corruption was rife and gangsters ruled the huge array of nightspots, gambling dens and bars catering for perversions of every sort.

Officers and ratings were treated to a series of lectures by the ship's doctors in the final few days before arrival. These were designed to shock and in many cases they did. The range of sexually transmitted diseases on offer ashore and the subsequent consequences were described in lurid detail. These lectures were followed by notices, and pamphlets circulated throughout the ship stressing how the excitement of a run ashore in Manila could quickly turn to fear and tragedy. As some were to discover, the sloe-eyed allure of a sexy and sinuous girl looking for a light from the nearby barstool could later turn quickly to something else entirely behind a brandished knife, or when introduced to a thuggish pimp.

Manila provided dives masquerading as bars with floorshows and private exhibitions that could cater for all tastes and which often competed with each other to reach new degrees of depravity in order to keep the cash registers in operation. Although the red light district of Manila was reckoned to have plumbed deep in the depravity industry, there was another nearby centre which could teach lessons to the entrepreneurs of Manila. Olongapo City had sprung up a few dozen years previously catering to the thousands of American servicemen based in or around the huge complex of Subic Bay. It was not a nice place – especially late at night.

This was actually my third visit to Manila so when leave was granted on the second afternoon of the visit, I strode off purposefully in the direction of an open space which had been turned into an art market. The breeze had dropped and the hot air of the city was becoming stifling. Every street seemed jammed from side to side with a seething, bustling mass of humanity. Colourful, noisy jeepneys of various sizes, all painted in garish colours and festooned with bells, decorations, ribbons and religious symbols, drove around the narrow streets carrying mixed loads of people, animals and goods. This was the bus and taxi service unique to the Philippines and, so we were told, provided a convenient haven for muggers, pickpockets and pimps. I walked.

I reached the art market and began to scout around. The array of pictures on offer was amazing. Many showed real talent but others were cheap and rather nasty. Nevertheless I had come to the right place. As I sized up the wares on offer I could see quite a few of my Australian colleagues, in several cases seemingly buying dozens of pictures, which would mean that they were then committed to employing some kind of help and transport to get their goodies back to the ship. Later on I learnt that there was a thriving and growing market in Sydney for these paintings – even the dodgy ones. After a while I identified four pictures that I thought typified what I was looking for. I haggled with two sellers for nearly an hour and after finally agreeing to pay in American dollars, I was able to hoist my burden and make my way back to the ship, rather more slowly than my outward journey. In fact although all of the paintings were framed two were quite small, and all of them were very carefully wrapped, leaving each with a string carrying handle.

As I made my way up the gangway I saw a new notice which declared that all Philippines wooden products including picture frames were contaminated with wood-boring beetles and other horrors. I contrived to saunter past the notice without seeing it and quickly disappeared to the sanctity of my cabin. At first I felt a little guilty but I have never seen a sign of any insect infestation in these picture frames and they all hang on my walls today.

I was still tucking my pictures away in my fairly spacious cabin when a single knock was followed by the partial opening of my cabin door, the gap being filled with Jim's luxuriant beard.

"Fancy a run ashore tonight?" he said enthusiastically. "Looks like it could be a squadron do. Not to be missed..." he tailed off as though he didn't actually believe what he had just said. I wasn't averse to a run ashore but with a dozen or so of Australia's finest all looking to light up Manila, things could develop and get out of hand.

We met in the bar at 6.30 sharp, a dozen of us. While 'flying speed' in all its liquid forms was being imbibed, an emissary was despatched to the gangway to see if there were any taxis hovering about – no jeepneys, he was told, just proper taxis. As the second round was being served he returned to report that the jetty was a throng of proper taxis and that he had personally selected and reserved three of them – to accompany us for the whole evening if so desired. This seemed like a good idea so we downed the last of the 'flying speed' and set off for the gangway, eagerly anticipating our transport and the night's entertainment. The taxis were old American models and at least one of them still retained a slight but distinct odour of stale vomit. I opened the window beside me a little further in the hope that the jungle smell of decaying vegetation from outside would mask the unpleasant smell from inside the vehicle. It didn't.

In a surprisingly short time we were cruising in convoy through the red light district where we were allegedly heading for a really smart, upmarket bar with "good cheap prices". As the convoy stopped a selection of touts and pimps materialised from out of nowhere and launched into their versions of high pressure marketing, dwelling on the number and quality of the girls, the power and cheapness of the booze and "floor shows like you never seen". Curiously they never mentioned the food or the service!

I stood beside the taxi still smelling slightly of stale vomit and looked around. On each side of the road glittering, flickering, neon signs in a variety of colours competed with one another to offer frequently bizarre services. Strip clubs, snake dancing clubs, topless bars, hostess bars, champagne bars (some chance!) floor shows, dirty bars, lap dancing bars (a whole new experience –it was claimed!), honky tonks, massage parlours and personal escort clubs were just a few of the services on offer.

We were deposited outside the recommended 'starter' bar and trooped through the plastic palm fringed entrance and into the dim interior. Everybody stopped, waiting for eyes to adjust to the dark atmosphere of the room. The place didn't seem very full, of people, that is. It was full of cigarette and cigar smoke overlaying sweat and cloying perfume. Adjusting to the light, I peered towards the bar where several patrons were perched on high stools, smoking and staring at the half empty glasses in front of them. Behind the bar stood a row of pretty young girls, giggling as they pulled handles to dispense half litres of foaming San Miguel beer. They were all naked from the waist up. For that matter they might also have been naked from the waist down as well, but the high bar counter protected their modesty in that direction. Our tall confident leader marched up to the bar and demanded "San Migs all round". Two of the girls sprang into action dispensing the beer. As each beer mug was placed on the bar in front of its owner, the girl would ask coquettishly, "You want dipped or no dipped?" I watched as the first couple of customers responded immediately.

"Dipped, please," they said exhibiting boyish enthusiasm. Without hesitation the barmaid leaned over the beer and lowered first one voluptuous brown breast then the other into the tankard of beer. The Archimedes principle came into effect as each breast displaced the beer which then joined the lake already spreading over the bar. I wondered how long it would take for the sticky beer to build up into a shiny hard mahogany crust on each of the sets of lithe, swinging boobs. When my beer was served, I politely declined the offer of a little extra sweat in it, whisking the glass away before the affronted barmaid could disobey me and dip it anyway. Some of the boys climbed up onto vacant bar stools and leered across at the semi-naked barmaids opposite. My companions were just sampling the 'San Mig' when I noticed one of our number, Billy, a young observer new to the squadron, who was leaning across the bar close to the girl on the other side who was now holding his hands and staring into his eyes. Other men clutched their beers and flopped into the collection of unmatched chairs scattered around small tables. As I dropped down into a chair long past its sell-by date the dingy little bar was suddenly illuminated by a bright light from above. Everybody stared up at what was now revealed as a glass ceiling. As we looked, a lissom suntanned woman strolled across the floor formed by the glass ceiling we were staring at. Apart from a pair of ridiculously high stiletto heels and shiny dark stockings, she was stark naked. When she reached the other side she picked up some sort of cloak and trailed it behind her. As the second crossing was completed the lights snapped out and we were left once more blinking and trying to accustom ourselves to the gloom. We had seen the floor show.

As my eyes once again penetrated the smoke and darkness I noticed that there was no sign of Billy. Both he and the girl had disappeared.

A few more beers were served but nothing else seemed to be happening. The bare-breasted barmaids had lost their initial sparkle, if that is what it could be called, and were now leaning against the bar gossiping with each other rather like bored housewives at a knitting circle. Nobody could understand what was being said behind the bar because the girls were speaking in Tagolog, the main Philippine language. The body language however – and there was plenty of body on display – suggested some degree of disappointment. The gang of happy Aussie sailors who had bounced through the door had not produced the expected boost to the evening's takings and worst of all there were no customers for 'extras'. But where was Billy? The boys were anxious to move on. There were more 'dives' to investigate, more horrible floorshows to see, more topless bars and – something becoming increasingly urgent – we were hungry and needed to find a place where the entertainment would be accompanied by food, hopefully exotic local food.

Two of Billy's closer friends went across to the bar to try to discover what had happened to Billy. Little sticky brown breasts were jiggled hopefully while their owners looked meaningfully at the near empty beer glasses. The anxious questioning continued but the barmaids seemed to have lost the ability to understand English. Lofty, our leader, in frustration, made a move towards the floor-length purple velvet curtain covering some sort of internal doorway. As he attempted to push the curtain aside it moved and he was faced with what was clearly the bouncer. The man stood a head taller than any of us except Lofty and was running to fat. His hair was greased up into a parody of Elvis Presley and the attempted impersonation was taken further by a spangly pink, draped jacket with velvet collar, open at the front but reaching almost to his knees. Skin-tight Levi jeans with a wide turn-up sitting on black suede thick-soled brothel creepers completed the ensemble. 'How apt,' I thought, looking at the shoes. Lofty had been stopped abruptly in his attempt to discover what lay beyond the curtain. He stared up at the bizarre apparition from a bygone age and then down at the eight inch long, wickedly narrow blade now held pointing towards his stomach. As if this was not warning enough, a second, mercifully slightly smaller but otherwise similar, thug sidled out of the darkness, as the bigger one, in the style of the old Western films, used his left hand to ease back the side of his jacket exposing the handle of what looked like an automatic pistol.

The room had gone awfully quiet and even seemed a little colder. All eyes, including those of the other customers seated in shadowy booths now seemed to be focussed upon the growing drama being played out in front of the scruffy curtain at the end of the bar. Lofty stood his ground and we heard the giant rumble "Fuck off, shit face," in a low hoarse and heavily accented voice. Lofty was unused to such ungracious greetings and stepped carefully back, eyes remaining focussed on the knife as more Australians began to shuffle forward, some clutching empty glasses. Trouble hovered over the room, but then, suddenly, the tense atmosphere was punctured as Billy, looking fresh and pink cheeked, grinning sheepishly, appeared from behind the two goons and said, "Hi Lofty."

It was time to leave and without discussion everybody walked away towards the door, leaving a scattering of half-filled glasses. As we left, curiously, several of these fell on to the floor, smashing and spilling beer to add to the layers already in the soiled carpet.

Our small fleet of taxis was parked in a row a few doors further along the road, the drivers standing smoking by the nearest one. They had not yet been paid so were unlikely to lose sight of their charges. A brief discussion took place alongside the cabs before we hopped in with the intention of heading down to the other end of the road in search of a smarter joint, better beer, suitable entertainment and above all, food. Five minutes later we piled out of the taxis as the doors were opened by liveried doormen. I wondered where they kept their guns – and their knives. We were ushered through into an altogether smarter place. It was busy and a wave of dance music drifted out as we drifted in. The entrance to the room was marked by a small cloakroom on each side, each counter being supervised by a pretty girl dressed in similar style to one of Hugh Hefner's 'Bunny Girls'. One was in gold with scarlet ears and the other was in silver with blue ears. "Very tasteful," said someone as the 'bunnies' smiled a toothy welcome and said, "Hi guys." My own appreciation of the welcome team was distracted by a prominent sign across the top of each 'cloakroom'. They said, in big bold letters 'PLEASE CHECK YOUR GUNS HERE. NO WEAPONS ALLOWED IN THE SALON'.

There was really no time to ponder this as we were escorted by two smiling clones of the gun-check girls towards two adjacent tables which were being hastily reassembled to form a big single table near the dance floor. I looked around and concluded that we had at least moved several notches up market from the previous establishment. The patrons seemed more lively, more local and on the whole well heeled. Couples were moving around, glued together on the small stage which was presently doing duty as a dance floor while a four-piece band knocked out its own peculiar version of a blues number. The place had atmosphere.

An incongruously blonde waitress dressed in a tight-fitting skimpy scarlet costume over long fishnet-covered legs, surmounted by a tray of cigars drifted out of the smoke haze dominating the upper half of the room. Everyone bought a cigar. A bottle masquerading as champagne arrived and was raucously waved away by my Australian companions to be replaced by frosted jugs of 'San Mig' beer, or at least, that's what was marked on the outside of the jugs. We puffed away at our fat Manila cigars and leaned back to watch the dance floor and wait for the floor show.

The lights dimmed, the dancers drifted back to tables or in the case of some of the girls, to seats around the bar and the music changed to a heavy persistent beat. A tall raven-haired girl shimmied across the small stage to a microphone stand which had just appeared and began to croon through a Carpenters number. Not many of her audience were concentrating on the song as she moved seductively around inside a clinging figure-hugging dress, which seemed unlikely to be able to continue to restrain her statuesque proportions. By the time the song had reached the third verse, her left hand was steadily slipping open small buttons down the side of the dress until with a quick turn the dress slid to the floor. The song was drowned in a roar of approval. She cruised steadily on through the song as first a lacy bra fell to her red stilettos followed by a couple of other lacy bits and pieces. The song ended and the curtain fell quickly as the singer stood legs and arms akimbo wearing only sheer black stockings which were connected to a lacy, wispy suspender belt by delicate little scarlet ribbon bows.

As the second stripper was reaching the conclusion of her slightly more sophisticated act Billy announced that he was going to pay for the first round of beer, despite the fact that there was a 'kitty' big enough to cater for the entire evening already in operation. He felt he owed it to us following the drama generated by his disappearance behind the scenes in the previous dive.

Billy was reaching for his wallet as our table waitress stood patiently by his side. After patting several pockets he pulled out a worn brown leather wallet shoved his hand inside it and then stopped, staring fixedly at the wallet and its contents. The blood drained from his face while the fingers of his other hand searched frantically through the compartments of this rather thin-looking wallet. The expression on Billy's face was moving rapidly through shock, anguish, horror and anger. "It's gone – it's all bloody gone," he grunted through clenched teeth while his facial expression alternated between outrage and despair diverting his nearest neighbours from the beginning of the next act, a slinky improbable blonde who was sliding out of a leopard skin catsuit by the process of peeling it away one tiny piece at a time.

Billy looked bereft as he waved the wallet about and repeated his assertion that he had been robbed, his previous drinks adding more volume to his outburst. As the rest of the table turned towards him he continued the tale of woe, "I had two hundred dollars U.S. in here, now there's barely twenty. That bitch robbed me," he wailed.

"What were you doing while she was robbing you, Billy?" I asked, innocently. Billy blushed and opened and shut his mouth. Then he said, "Taking a shower – afterwards, you know," he finished lamely.

"Wow, Billy," responded Tom. "She was just charging you a bit more than you thought. At least she left you a taxi fare – that seems considerate."

"Yeah, tell us Billy, was she good, really good?"

"Was she worth two hundred bucks Billy?"

"Was that bucks you said?"

"Always take yer wallet outa yer strides when you drop 'em Billy."

Ignoring the ribaldry and joking at his expense, Billy continued the sad story. "It must have been when I took the shower," he repeated again, as though we had not heard the first time. This produced a wave of snorting, choking laughter around the table.

"Don't say you fell for that one!"

"Hey, the Sheila's left you yer bus fare – now that's what I call professional. A real decent working girl." And so the banter rolled on while Billy became quieter and concentrated on his beer. Gerry intervened by ordering another round.

The laughter around the table had died away to the former conversational buzz punctuated by one or two beery remarks directed towards the ladies of the floor show who were reaching the end of an uninspiring dance routine – uninspiring because they still had most of their clothes on – when the louche atmosphere of the nightclub was disturbed by angry voices from across the room. The act rolled on having lost the attention of almost all of the audience as most heads turned toward a table on the opposite side of the room where three or four sharp-suited men were standing, chairs thrown back arguing furiously, fingers jabbing the air. Another man, diminutive in a white dinner jacket, attempted to intervene and was swept to one side by an angry gesture from one of the protagonists. The stage act ended and the three dancers wandered away. Nobody noticed. The clients were now focussed on the small man who was picking himself up from the floor and backing away from the argument. Suddenly, he lunged forward, light flashing on a blade in his hand before he plunged it into the side of the man who had struck him. Then the band music, which had almost died away, was shattered by a single gunshot. The music stopped, the performers disappeared and all around the room customers dived under tables or lay on the floor. No one seemed to have been shot but the man who had been stabbed was thrashing around on the floor making a lot of noise. Three more gunshots came in quick succession. Then a dozen or so more, from various directions. Bullets thudded into walls and ricocheted off metalwork. Still, no one seemed to have been shot. I looked across under the table at my companions, who were, I noticed with some surprise, already moving across the carpet in flat Indian-style crawls, heading for a door marked 'Exit'. It didn't take us long to get out of there. As the exit door swung back into place behind me I could hear the sounds of the battle being joined by a sizeable contingent of the local police. Whistles, more gunshots, pained yells and sounds of splintering furniture from behind the door suggested that the party was really getting into its stride. So much for checking their weapons at the entrance!

We had emerged into some sort of box room. That is to say, it seemed to be filled with dozens of discarded cardboard boxes. Indian file, we followed the narrow corridor between the piles of boxes towards another door at the far end. It was not locked but was secured by two bolts on the inside. They seemed to be rusted into position but a couple of boots applied with adrenaline and nervous energy soon solved that.

Emerging through the door into the night we were in a filthy alley between two buildings. Discarded fast food packaging, cans and empty bottles competed with used condoms and cardboard for space the paving. The alley led to the front road where hopefully we would find our taxis. At the end of the alley a young prostitute was enthusiastically plying her trade, skirt hitched high around her waist, with a white-suited American sailor. He looked briefly at us without deviating from the task in hand as we lurched out onto the pavement and looked around for our taxis. Billy was still moaning about his misfortune. Someone, in an attempt to shut him up said, "Never mind Bill, she may have left you a dose instead." Billy became silent. In the distance a blue U.S. Navy open jeep filled with U.S. Navy patrolmen – 'Snowdrops' – was hurtling out of a side street and turning in our direction. Police and dark-suited men were scuffling in the doorway of the club a few yards along to the right. It was time to leave. As one we turned sharply left, away from the area of activity and it was with some relief that our distinctive yellow taxis appeared, parked in the next side street.

We tried two more examples of Manila's night life. One was a half-hearted front for a brothel. The other offered slightly more interesting entertainment, including such exotic luxuries as lap dancing. "You can look, but you not touch anything seee, Honeee," and pole dancing. We looked, we didn't touch and as the evening wore on the repetitive entertainment became boring and we became more and more hungry. As funds ran low and the night moved into the early hours a decision was reached that we needed to find some reasonably priced food outlet. Thus it was that at about half past two that morning a weary bunch of Anglo-Australian adventurers looking somewhat soiled and bedraggled tumbled out of three taxis to join the crowd of late night diners standing around a mobile food bar at the end of the dock piers. The perfect end to a run ashore in Manila.

****

Two days later, *Melbourne* was due to sail for Singapore in the early afternoon. Before that I was scheduled to lead a two aircraft sortie to the small U.S. Navy airfield at Cubi Point near Subic Bay where both aircraft were to undergo compass swings. This would take several hours after which I was to lead the aircraft out to join up with the ship at sea as it steamed down the coast.

The two aircraft were brought up and ranged on deck and we were away into the pleasantly cool morning by seven a.m. We formed up into a loose echelon and climbed to a thousand feet heading towards the harbour entrance, passing the fortress island of Corregidor before turning north to fly along the deep green jungle covered Philippines coast towards the sprawling American naval base at Subic Bay. The increasing intensity of the Vietnam War had driven a very considerable expansion of the Subic Bay naval base, which together with the equally impressive US. Air Force Base at Clark Field and the adjacent U.S. Marine Corps facilities had been the catalyst for the expansion of the onetime village of Olongapo into the rolling, glitzy, money churning, gangster-dominated Olongapo City. It was, I had been told by a taciturn Australian, "A condominium of brothels built over an open sewer, with a few casinos and saloons added for variety."

The description was probably a little harsh but not a long way from the truth. The village had expanded as rapidly as the local builders could shove up the rickety buildings and attach the garish signs and neon lights. The whole project was fuelled by the thousands of American servicemen who were posted back to the Philippines from Vietnam for rest and recreation, with money in their pockets and a need to let their hair down. I believe that one reason for *Melbourne* being sent to Manila rather than Subic was

191

the perceived need to keep the volatile and expressive Aussies away from the equally volatile returning Americans.

In fact a previous visit by the carrier had produced an incident which had led to a major but thankfully temporary rupture in diplomatic relations between the two allied nations. Some American military bases can seem a little flamboyant in the way they decorate the entrances to their establishments. One such was a United States Marines Corps outpost between Subic and Manila. The entrance to this base was formed by a tall granite arch. Across the top of this arch was a bold and uncompromising statement carved into the stone. It said 'Beneath these Portals Pass the Finest Fighting Men in the World'. Someone had added to this grandiose assertion 'and some Americans'. This had been carefully but prominently painted in thick black paint. The U.S. Marines, who can be sensitive about such things even at the best of times, had alleged that the desecration was the work of Australian sailors and had simultaneously launched a sense of humour failure of epic proportions. Confrontation and, later, small battles had taken place between men of the two nationalities who had encountered each other in the dives of Manila and Olongapo. The visiting Aussies had flatly refused to acknowledge guilt but they had generously offered to pay for the removal of the offending remark and the restoration of the gateway to its former glory. The Australian denial of responsibility had been grudgingly accepted but it was difficult to see who else might have carried out the job – and who else could have achieved it under the noses of the American guards without being caught?

While the observers and the aircrewmen were busily getting on with the compass swings one of the co-pilots set off in the direction of the PX with a list of purchases to be made on behalf of his colleagues. The Navy PX at Subic was supposed to be one of the cheapest in the world, but then I reflected, all of the PXs seemed to come with the reputation of being the cheapest in the world. With nothing to do for the next three or four hours I wandered off with the remaining two pilots in the direction of the big ship berths at Subic to take a closer look at some of the U.S. Navy's newer fleet units. Strolling and admiring the arrangements on a big Iwo Jima class helicopter carrier, my attention was drawn by an even bigger ship coming in from the entrance to the bay, trailing smoke and going a bit fast for such a big ship, or any ship, to be entering harbour. We quickened our pace and moved towards the empty dockside berth that the ship seemed to be heading for, only to find our progress blocked by heavy steel barriers with baton-wielding Marines posted on the other side. With the story of the previous difficulty still uppermost in our minds we had spent most of our first hour after arrival at Cubi Point keeping well clear of the bullet-headed Marines seen moving about within the base, so now, my little group sheared off away from the barriers, overcoming the problem by climbing up onto some higher ground which afforded a nice view of the rapidly approaching ship and the preparations made to receive it.

We settled down quietly and unobtrusively to watch. Nobody came to disturb us. Looking down I could see rows of heavy duty trucks, some khaki painted buses, at least thirty ambulances and a group of military police custody vehicles. As the ship crunched none too gently alongside, heaving lines snaked out from the forecastle and the quarterdeck. They were quickly snatched up by uniformed Marines, attached to heavier mooring ropes and hauled back inboard. The whole thing was an exercise in efficiency and within only a few minutes the ship was moored fore and aft. A few vehicle engines started up and groups of Marines appeared on the jetty. I couldn't at first work out what they were dressed in and how they were equipped. Then I saw that they were wearing the same type of clothing that riot police wear. They were carrying axe-handle type sticks so it became apparent pretty quickly that their intention was to sort somebody out.

Two unusual vehicles appeared from among the parked lorries and started reversing smartly towards the ship. Each vehicle looked rather like the portable exit ramps that are driven up to airliners at some airports to allow passengers to disembark from the aircraft. In this case they headed for the ship's side adjacent to two entry points beneath the flight deck. The groups of baton-armed Marines were running behind the trucks and as soon as the vehicles came to a stop the Marines swarmed aboard, up the steeply sloping ramps and disappeared into the ship. Nothing much happened for the next half an hour and I believed that the show was over. I had just announced that it was time to make our way back to the aircraft when the show started again. We all paused, watching. Some of the first Marines to board the ship were appearing on the makeshift gangways herding battered-looking sailors before them. Two mobile cranes appeared, inching slowly towards the ship each with a long gangway dangling underneath the jib. Fire hoses could be seen playing somewhere around the base of the 'island'. Ambulances revved up and moved towards the ship. More Marines poured in and still others emerged. Some medics now entered the ship and as the initial excitement began to die down larger numbers of distraught and battered-looking sailors began to file down the gangways, some with hands tied or handcuffed. They were made to sit on the concrete dockside while individuals were identified and taken over to the custody vehicles. Stretchers were being removed from the ship as some ship's officers came down on to the dockside to be met by other more senior officers who had arrived in grey Navy cars. Almost as quickly as the drama had begun, it all drew to a close. The remaining vehicles parked on the dockside started to drive away and when we left even the barriers had been removed. It looked just like a typical dockyard scene. A large aircraft carrier, sitting gently alongside the pier, waiting for instructions.

Later I learnt more of what I had witnessed that afternoon, although, I am sure, not the whole story. An Essex class carrier, operating on the flight line off the coast of Vietnam at readiness to provide air support to the troops ashore, had suffered a serious race riot. The conflagration on board had been three ways with Whites, Blacks and Hispanics all fighting each other. With some difficulty, the Bridge, the engine rooms and boiler rooms and the Combat Information Centre (what we call the Operations Room) had been secured and held. The various factions had launched themselves on a damage spree throughout the other parts of the carrier. The ship had left the flight line and steamed back to Subic Bay as fast as possible. We had seen the rest.

****

By early afternoon, compass swings were complete, I had visited the Navy Air Operation Centre and filed the necessary flight plan, we were manned up and had approval to taxi. I had carried out a crew briefing before manning the aircraft, observed quite a lot of packages from the PX being loaded into the cabin of the second aircraft and Chris, the observer in my crew had obtained an estimated rendezvous position from our ship. We taxied out onto the short helicopter runway, rolled a few feet forward and lifted simultaneously into the hover. A quick check of vital signs within the cockpit and I pushed the nose forward, increasing the 'collective' power as we climbed sedately away with the second aircraft following faithfully in a close port echelon. We kept the tight formation until we approached the edge of the Subic Military Air Traffic Zone then I opened the formation out to conserve fuel and allow everybody to relax. *Melbourne's* approach frequency was selected on the radio and the formation turned south to parallel

195

the coast while the pilots peered ahead to locate the ship. Several calls were made to the ship but the radio remained obstinately silent.

I believed that we would have about an hour to run down the coast, having first passed Corregidor and the wide mouth of Manila Bay. An hour passed without any response to our UHF radio calls either on the carrier's approach frequency or on the local frequency. *Melbourne* was not where she ought to be and was not talking to us. Additionally, Tacan did not seem to be working. Not being in the right rendezvous position was almost a competitive sport with aircraft carriers but refusing to answer our increasingly earnest bleats on the radio was more worrying. I reduced the speed of the formation to conserve fuel and started my own mental computation of where we might go if we were unable to locate the carrier. Options were limited. We were too far from Subic or Cubi Point to attempt to return there and although we might make it back to Manila I wasn't sure how nicely we would be received if we unexpectedly arrived without radio communication (we had UHF but commercial airfields operated VHF). The third option was to turn and fly straight inshore from this position to try to find a suitable landing site, avoid the gathering thunderheads, and prevent the locals from stealing the aircraft one piece at a time. All the options were bad and I had just decided on a compromise, to turn back up the coast towards Manila for as long as the fuel would allow before flying inland to try to find a landing site closer to civilisation, when the Tacan needle spun round and the radio crackled into life.

The Tacan readout suggested that with a slight turn to starboard away from the coast, the ship would be about fifteen miles ahead of us. Gently, I eased the cyclic column forward to increase speed and as I did so the radio operator on the ship dropped his bombshell.

"Blue formation this is Mother. We have a major fire on board and cannot receive you back aboard. You are to return alongside and carry out a controlled ditching. Be advised the ship may have difficulty in manoeuvring."

Was this a sick joke? Was some sadistic bastard on board having me on?

"I can see a ship ahead," said the co-pilot. "Looks like the carrier."

"Zulu Kilo, this is Blue Leader," I snarled into the radio with as much force as I could. "Your last transmission not understood. Say again, over."

"Blue Leader, I say again, we are on fire and you are to return alongside and carry out a controlled ditching."

"Fuck that for a box of soldiers," came a voice from the cabin. I sympathised.

"Blue two go private," I transmitted as I selected the squadron private frequency.

"Blue Two on private."

"Did you copy all that crap?" I said.

"Unbelievable," came the response.

"What's your fuel state?" I asked.

"Six hundred pounds."

That was a little less than my own fuel state but enough for at least a further twenty-five minutes' flying. The coastline was beginning to look more inviting by the second and I reckoned we could find somewhere flat enough to land near the gently sloping beach. I switched back to the ship's frequency.

"I can see the ship clearly," said my co-pilot, drawing me back to our present circumstances. "We have five miles to run and I can see a lot of smoke."

"OK," I acknowledged, then to the ship, "Zulu Kilo this is Blue Leader, both aircraft have sufficient fuel for at least twenty minutes, confirm that you do not wish me to turn inshore in an attempt to save the aircraft and that you wish me to ditch alongside."

"Blue leader, Zulu Kilo, rejoin to hover on the port beam and prepare to ditch," came the response.

"Well that was pretty bloody stupid," I said to my crew in general. Then, into the radio, "Two, go private." The co-pilot switched frequencies.

"Blue two, Boss," I heard through the headset.

"The plan is this," I said into the radio, "we will reduce to fifty knots and enter a gentle line astern orbit to port of the ship. Call at one hundred and fifty pounds of fuel then ditch, power on, into wind, not aligned with the ship. Got that?"

"Got it. Back to local."

I switched back to the ship's frequency, clicked the transmit button to show my number two that I was on frequency but said nothing. I was full of contempt for the apparently inept handling of the emergency and because of their incompetence I would be taking a swim.

The minutes ticked by and I watched the fuel needles easing inevitably back around the faces of the dials. No one spoke. Then with two hundred pounds of fuel indicated, about six minutes' flying time, the voice emerged from the radio, this time full of confidence. "Blue Formation you are cleared to land – acknowledge."

I pressed the button and said, "Blue Leader, Roger. You go first – Two."

Without pausing the other aircraft swept past, astern and above me, turning in towards the flight deck. Thirty seconds later I was touching down on the spot behind him.

****

I made my way down towards the briefing room with some difficulty. Having been instructed to ditch my aircraft in a remote tropical sea with the nearest shore likely to be bandit ridden I was not in the best frame of mind. However as I clambered over fire hoses and sloshed through several inches of filthy water swilling about the decks with smoke-blackened bulkheads and the smell of burning rubber adding to the scene of confusion and devastation my mood began to ease. Clearly the ship had suffered a major fire and minds would have been focussed on the immediate problems of avoiding total destruction. Progress through the ship was further disrupted by watertight doors and hatches being firmly clipped shut and numerous damage control parties with blackened faces and wet overalls trying to clear up their equipment. The main lighting system was out and the whole scene was made even more dramatic by the dim emergency lights which in some areas seemed also to have been damaged. Electricians were dragging temporary power cables along the decks and working to recover supplies lost to the fire.

Eventually I made it through the door into the briefing room. Apart from having only half the lights working this room seemed at first sight to be remarkably undamaged. On closer inspection I saw that the paint on the inboard bulkhead was blistered and the bulkhead itself looked slightly distorted. Apart from the sub-lieutenant duty officer the briefing room was empty. I passed into the adjacent locker room which had even less serviceable lighting, took off my Mae West and stowed it away with my helmet and other kit before returning to the briefing room to complete the flight paperwork. I wondered whether the coffee urn was still functioning. It wasn't but it still had enough warm water to provide some sort of a 'brew' for the eight crew members now flopped in the chairs. We gathered that the fire had started from some sort of electrical fault but had spread quickly. The ship had gone to Emergency Stations and the whole thing had lasted for about an hour and a half before being finally extinguished. The sections most affected were accommodation and administration but some consequent water damage had occurred within the hangar due to 'damping down'. Water had been sprayed around the periphery of the hangar to keep the area cool. With six Tracker aircraft all filled with high octane petrol, not to mention ready to use stores of grease, oils and other highly volatile and combustible items such as a few bombs in the magazines, it was necessary to keep the major compartment as cool as possible. If the fire had spread into the hangar the ship would most probably have been lost.

There seemed nothing else for me in the briefing room so I finished my barely warm coffee, gathered up my things and ventured out into the still chaotic corridor where I sloshed my way slowly along towards my cabin.

My cabin had fared surprisingly well. The door was smoke-blackened but inside everything seemed relatively normal. The bulkheads were streaked with traces of smoke in places and the carpet was soaked but the emergency light inside the door was working and, most important, my bunk was undamaged. There was no air conditioning or ventilation so the cabin seemed hot and stuffy. Nevertheless it was home so I opened up my folding aluminium chair and flopped down into it. A few minutes later the door eased open and Jim's bearded face peered in. "Welcome back!" he said. "I thought we'd finally got rid of you."

"No chance," I said. "What now?"

Jim eased himself into the other chair and told me what I had already heard about the fire. We discussed some of my thoughts about being told to ditch my aircraft. I pointed out that even when under attack during the Second World War aircraft carriers did everything possible to recover their aircraft.

We continued to chat about this and that for the next couple of hours, during which time the Ship's Main Broadcast was restored and various announcements guided the carrier back to a near normal state. By dinner time I had achieved a cold shower and had some ventilation air once more emerging from the 'punkah louvres' in my cabin although it came out hot because the air conditioning was still off. In fact, we were never again to experience the luxury of air conditioning during the remaining deployment.

Curiously, I cannot remember any member of the hierarchy of the Air Group or the ship saying anything to me about the ill-considered and peremptory instructions to ditch the two aircraft in my returning section, nor making any comment about my repeated refusal to obey the unwise commands.

Chapter 17

Singapore

We were scheduled to take part in a joint tactical exercise with the United States Navy starting in the next few days, so flying operations were reduced while the whole ship's company tried to repair the damage caused by the fire. The Air Group cleaned and cosseted the aircraft and the hangar, working hard to eliminate the knock-on effects of salt water having been liberally sprayed around during the fire. By the time the exercise started the ship had recovered most of the lost systems – except the air conditioning – had replaced damaged pipes and cables, restored lighting and generally cleaned the place up. The ten days or so of the exercise passed fairly quickly as we trundled around the pre-arranged track in the ocean fending off attacks from above and below the surface. My logbook shows a steady series of anti-submarine screening sorties punctuated by the inevitable planeguard stints. Thoughts began to turn towards the delights awaiting us in Singapore, which were expected to be many and diverse.

We weren't set up for a ceremonial entry into Singapore, which would anyway have been fairly pointless because we were to be berthed in the old Royal Navy dockyard in the north of the island. First though, we had been invited to be a VIP demonstration platform for an impressive group of important local chaps. I never found out exactly who they were because once again the information supply from the Command was sparse.

The equatorial heat was oppressive despite the light offshore breeze as *Melbourne* slowed to a few knots just to the south of the rows of tankers and freighters waiting to enter the Port of Singapore. Three small Iroquois helicopters appeared to the north of the ship in line astern formation. They all wore Singapore Air Force markings and were clearly headed for our ship. Following each other around the stern, they flew slowly up the flight deck and landed, apparently taking little notice of the director's signals. Each aircraft deposited about six or seven men onto the deck, who were quickly gathered up and guided towards the 'island'. As soon as the passengers were clear, the three aircraft lifted uncertainly into the air and followed each other forward over the bows before turning in the direction of Singapore. The new arrivals were a mixture of civilians and men in uniform, some in army green and some in air force blue. The civilians all seemed to be dressed in identical dark blue lightweight suits, white shirts and dark sober ties.

The party was ushered down to the wardroom to meet the Admiral, Captain, Squadron Commanders and one or two other important chaps over coffee and delicate pastries, while 'upstairs' on the flight deck, Trackers and helicopters were brought up from the hangar and launched as soon as pre-take off preparations were complete. Three Skyhawks were then brought up, manned up and ranged behind the island, ready to start engines.

The important visitors were led up to the Bridge and the best 'goofer' positions nearby, while we who were airborne took station in pre-designated positions each to await our turn in the flying demonstrations about to take place.

One after the other the three Skyhawks were boosted off the catapult in a cascade of smoke, steam and sound. As they climbed away ahead of the ship, I came nipping in from my waiting position astern, flaring dramatically to a hover abeam the port bow and immediately lowering the sonar body. As the body hit the surface of the water the shadows of three Trackers passed over me. They drew away ahead and I could see that they were maintaining an impressively tight formation. The ship was already passing me and the important guests would soon lose sight – or more likely – lose interest in me so I invited my crew to recover the sonar body. The VIPs now had something more interesting to attract their attention, as two of the jets came screaming in, low level, from ahead, opening their formation sufficiently to pass down either side of the carrier, and causing my helicopter to rock alarmingly in the turbulence created by their slipstream. I had no time to think about my proximity to the jets because the third one came roaring through from the opposite direction, again passing close above me. A plaintive voice crackled over the intercom:

"Fuck this for a box of soldiers," said my crewman. "I reckon we fuck off outa here, sharpish, Boss."

"We're on our way," I said as I pulled in power, shoved the nose down and accelerated away from the ship, turning hard left as I did so. The next helicopter pulled up from low down on the blind side of the ship, passed speedily down the length of the ship from forward to aft and pulled up into an impressive sequence of 'wing-overs' before diving back down over the stern to hold off once again on the blind side.

The display by the Air Group continued for another ten minutes with each type of aircraft showing off its special tricks before the whole thing was concluded with a combined flypast by the nine aircraft taking part.

It all seemed to go quite well and I hoped the visitors were duly impressed. But I never knew how the display was received because once again nobody bothered to tell us, the 'poor bloody (airborne) infantry'.

Most of the ship's company actually seemed to view the display for the Singaporean guests as a time-wasting exercise unreasonably preventing them from getting ashore and sampling all the goodies Singapore had to offer.

We seemed to spend the rest of that morning threading our track through the shipping waiting offshore and slowly feeling our way towards the former Royal Naval Dockyard facing the causeway at Sembawang on the north side of the island.

After the fleshpots of Manila, most of the sailors venturing ashore were somewhat limited in what they could get up to and in any case there were other limitations imposed by the Government of Singapore. Lee Kwan Yu, the long-serving and somewhat inflexible Prime Minister, had set in place rules to control his population which some might have suggested would be better suited to the Prussian Guard. However, it seemed to work. The crime rate was very low and the whole island was clean, litter-free and tidy. Men with overly long hairstyles were risking jail so short back and sides was the order of the day and therefore the local fellows looked pretty smart. The Singapore Government had not yet introduced the policy of providing each new arrival in the country with a black-edged welcome card casually explaining that the penalty for being found in possession of drugs was death but a smiling man in a black suit and short haircut did come on board to address groups of the ship's company, providing the same rather uncompromising message. Nobody took even an aspirin ashore.

Singapore was also considered by most sailors to be one of the world's best 'Rabbit Runs'. 'Rabbit' is the term used for any item purchased ashore in a foreign port, usually to be showered upon loved ones on returning home but sadly often quite useless to the recipient. A 'Rabbit Run' was therefore a 'run ashore' for the purpose of buying 'rabbits'. In the hustle and bustle of a naval life, good intentions sometimes get lost on the way and not infrequently, shore-going expeditions intended as rabbit runs ended up with the only purchases achieved having been served in a glass.

This was the time before credit cards were in general use; sailors were paid mostly in cash and few of them owned cheque books. So an inadvertent diversion of a 'rabbit run' into an expensive 'haircut run' or worse meant that the sailor either had to stay on board for the rest of the visit or borrow from a messmate – this being officially frowned upon and, if discovered, likely to merit formal sanctions for both parties.

I wanted to get hold of some Noritake china to add to a set I had bought on a previous trip to Singapore. The best place for this was in Change Alley, a meandering covered market down in the centre of the city, near the waterfront. Since I expected to be carrying heavy parcels on the way back my plan was to take a bus down to the city and ride back in one of the smart air conditioned taxis. Bus rides in Singapore always offered interesting experiences. Some of the vehicles were quite modern but many were rather ramshackle and the buses were likely to divert away from the official route to drop off groups of passengers nearer their homes, especially if they had livestock with them. The small pigs and crated chickens sharing my bus with me were in fact quite civilised and barely interrupted the conversation which flowed around me.

The bus ride was a social occasion and as I sat surrounded by a blaze of coloured shirts and dresses, I was politely included in the conversation.

"Have you been to Singapore before?" asked the smiling middle-aged man seated across the aisle from me.

"Oh yes," I said, "several times."

"What do you think of our country?" he said.

"Very nice, very clean," I responded enthusiastically. The smiles that appeared on the Indian, Malay and Chinese faces surrounding me suggested that it was the right answer.

"Have you heard of our Prime Minister, Mr Lee Kwan Yu?" said a batik-clad lady leaning round from the seat in front.

"Oh yes," I said. "Mr Lee Kwan Yu is very well known."

"What do you think of our Prime Minister?" This came from the original inquisitor.

"He is a most effective and highly successful man who has done much for his country," I said very carefully, fixing a stern expression on my face. I realised that once again I had said the right thing as a little round of applause twittered around the centre of the bus where I was sitting. My new friends seemed satisfied and lapsed into local gossip for the rest of the journey. I had passed. I was not going to be thrown into jail without passing 'Go'.

Shopping in Singapore was, and despite the development of a skyscraper city, probably still is, a fascinating experience. The shops and stalls running through Change Alley will sell almost anything but every purchase must follow a pattern. The customer will arrive, stroll around looking for his intended purchases on several stalls. Eventually a discussion will ensue and when this leads to serious business, a chair or stool will appear and ice cold soft drinks will be delivered by small boys. The purchase does not necessarily have to be completed during the first visit and, sometimes, it can take weeks.

In fact I knew where I was going on this occasion and when I reached the small open fronted shop, pausing to declare the purpose of my visit I was welcomed like a long-lost friend. It took an hour to socialise around my decision making before I left the shop to parcel up my new crockery while I wandered happily through the amazing array of merchandise on offer in the other shops and stalls nearby.

I loaded my packages into the smart yellow and black taxi before slipping into the back seat. I had already negotiated a reasonable fare so I settled back luxuriating in the delight of air conditioning, briefly closing my eyes.

"What do you think of our country?" said the driver from the front seat.

"Very nice, very clean," I replied.

"Have you heard of our Prime Minister?" The driver turned his head to look into the back seat, narrowly missing a heavily laden cart drawn by a donkey.

"Oh yes, Mr Lee Kwan Yu is very well known." The conversation was beginning to sound familiar.

"What do you think of our Prime Minister?"

"He is a most successful and highly respected man who has done much for his country." I thought it best to stick to the recommended script and thus avoid being trundled round to the nearest cop shop.

The rest of the trip passed in relative silence as I luxuriated in the now unfamiliar coolness of air conditioning while surveying the passing scenery and the back of my driver's beautifully tonsured head, which conformed to the officially approved style.

****

I carried my purchases down to my cabin and stowed them away as securely as I could before strolling off to the bathrooms for a shower before the pre-dinner crowd arrived. When I returned to the cabin I turned up the air flow from the 'punkah louvre' ventilators as much as I could and wrapped myself in a towel waiting in the slightly vain hope that the humid Singaporean air being pumped into the cabin would enable me to achieve a state of at least partial dryness. While sitting there I finished off a letter home before changing once more and ambling slowly off in the direction of the wardroom.

There was still an hour or so before dinner and the wardroom was fairly quiet. Most of the officers present were, like me, dressed in casual civilian clothes – the occasional uniformed individual indicating that the holder was nominated for some duty function. I wrote out a bar chit for a large beer, and waited while the single steward on duty got around to it, hoping that the beer would be well chilled by the time it arrived. It was. I collected my beer with a pleasing frost already showing on the outside of the glass, searched around to see if I could find a newspaper, found the previous day's *Singapore Times*, and settled myself quietly in a corner seat to drink my beer and while away the time reading the inconsequential local news in yesterday's paper.

Presently other officers, mostly unknown to me, drifted into the bar, ordered drinks and started chatting. I found myself progressively distracted from my newspaper as I picked up more and more of the conversation around the expanding group at the bar. Someone plumped down on the seat beside me and I looked around to see Jim manoeuvring his beard round the rim of an enticing-looking tankard of beer.

"Been ashore?" he said as he emerged from the beer.

"Yeah, got my Noritake and a few things," I replied, still watching the group at the bar. Jim took another swig and we both watched and listened to our brother officers in silence for a few moments. The dominant subject of the conversation was Singapore and the relative success, or lack of it, of the various individuals who had been 'rabbit running' ashore. We both noted with interest that the usual subjects of conversation around the bar – women, booze, horse racing and the iniquities of the Navy had been displaced. This suggested that most of our companions were experiencing Singapore for the first time. Experienced hands tended simply to take Singapore, or Hong Kong which was viewed in a similar way, for what it was. A run ashore was a carefully planned expedition to a well known and well researched establishment for the purchase, after firm but good-natured haggling, of whatever goods were appropriate to the area or the particular business. The villages of Changi, Seletar, Nee Soon, Sembawang, and Johore Bahru in Malaysia were visited as well as Change Alley and some of the smart shops in the city where good prices could also be achieved by the application of the same barter technique used in the less sophisticated outlets. The novices could easily be spotted by the traders for what they were which occasionally resulted in a certain amount of sadness occurring upon the discovery of some defect in recently purchased goods, usually after the ship had sailed.

One of the Tracker observers had arrived and joined the group at the bar. Tall and well built, he was a very self-confident young man ready to give an authoritative opinion on almost any subject and frequently found to be way out of his depth. This evening he was clearly happy with life and demonstrating this by the volume of his voice and his willingness to include anyone within earshot in his circle. He was expounding the advantages of patronising a previously unknown tailor on the far side of the village of Seletar. He was dressed in a fairly snug-fitting long-sleeved safari suit fashioned in a dark tan material which was right up to date and, presumably, the work of his newfound tailor.

One of the things that an experienced shopper will look for in purchasing any tailoring in Singapore is the quality and strength of the cotton thread used to hold the item together. The man in the new safari suit did not appear to have been aware of this small but essential point when he went shopping. Standing well back from the bar to avoid any spillage on his lovely new suit he was really getting into his subject. Gesticulating and waving his arms he was now dominating the diminishing group surrounding him as he related once again the finer points of his tailor. Jim and I sat fascinated by the performance taking place in front of us. I had noticed that with each expansive gesture of the left arm a small but noticeable distortion was becoming evident where the sleeve met the shoulder of the jacket. The distortion became a tiny gap. A piece of thread appeared, then another, as the tiny slit-like gap began to open up to indicate a parting of the ways between the sleeve and the rest of the jacket. The bottom end of the sleeve had begun to crinkle up against the vast dome like chronometer worn on his left wrist so our raconteur had not yet noticed anything untoward. But his small audience had, and constrained expressions

211

of shock and mirth began to follow each other around the assembled faces. By this time the gap between shoulder and sleeve could not be ignored and a significant number of the occupants of the room had stopped whatever they were doing or saying to stare fixedly at this unusual example of a Singaporean tailor's work. The focal point of all the eyes in the wardroom suddenly realised he was just that and, glancing down, he realised the full horror of his predicament as the lower end of the independent sleeve finally found its way past the huge wrist-mounted chronometer and having overcome the obstruction continued on its way to the carpet. The owner of the sleeve banged down his glass and fled.

I heard later that at the same time that the safari suit had been purchased, a dozen made-to-measure shirts had also been bought. These were beautifully wrapped and presented in clear film packages, as are most shirts. However, on opening, the shirts were found to consist solely of a collar and a shirt front with nothing else. Several of the Tracker Squadron officers accompanied their shirtless, suit-less colleague back to Seletar village to seek redress but on arrival they found that the business had closed up and disappeared.

Another example of unfortunate purchasing came to me some time after we had sailed from Singapore. I happened upon a touching little ceremony as something was being consigned to the deep from one of the port side gun sponsons. It was a vacuum cleaner, I was told. One of our squadron sailors had determined to buy a state of the art vacuum cleaner of the pull-along type to take home as a present for his Mum. Every day he had visited a particular shop in Nee Soon village which specialised in domestic appliances. On the first day he had chosen the machine he wanted and had then begun a protracted negotiation over the price. He was a hard bargainer, and daily, over iced tea or a soft drink, he would sit down with the shop proprietor and shave a little bit more off the price, as they both admired the shiny red machine set out before them. The afternoon before we sailed from Singapore he visited the shop for the last time, tried his luck once more and was surprised by a generous final reduction in the price. He shook hands with the proprietor, settled up with the last half of the payment and picked up the parcel which had been superbly wrapped and protected to withstand the rigours of the journey to Australia in the corner of a ship's store room. The proprietor smilingly waived any charge for the additional packaging, wishing the new owner many happy years of service from his machine. The young man was so proud of his achievement that after another week at sea he could not resist taking one more look at his purchase. Carefully opening the upper layers of packaging he peered into the box. Something didn't look right so, with some difficulty he reached in and prized the cleaner out of its box. The first thing he noticed was that there were no tools. The second thing was that, running from end to end on the underside of the casing was a wide crack. The third thing was that it would only operate on one hundred and fifty volts, the electricity supply used in the United States. Finally he saw, lying in the bottom of the box, a handwritten note. It read: 'This may not be exactly what you are expecting, kind sir, but it is the only item in my shop which justifies the tiny amount of money you were prepared to pay me.'

Before we left Singapore I made a few more purchases including a watch for Irene, another for myself and some presents for my family. I had just walked back through the dockyard with these things in various bags and packages, trailed by the regular pack of rather unnerving pi-dogs that appeared whenever work in the dockyard ended for the day when I was hailed and reminded that a squadron run ashore was scheduled for that evening. Since it was likely to provide less excitement and more amusement than the run ashore in Manila – in addition to being less expensive, I decided to go along.

We assembled in the bar at six, sank a couple of beers to keep the electrolytic levels right and under a cloud of umbrellas we all filed off through the usual evening downpour and the huge puddles in the direction of the dockyard gate. Several taxis, rather ramshackle in relation to the smart shiny ones down in the city, were quickly filled to capacity by the first half of our group and rumbled off trailing smoke in a generally southerly direction. I waited with the remainder of the team in the hope that the drivers would pass the word to their colleagues – those that had radios – or that others would pass by looking for trade.

The rain had stopped and a debate had started over whether we should seek solace in a local bar, wait for the taxis or search for a bus, when the first of three vehicles struggled up the slight incline and stopped, drivers peering out and smiling expectantly. We piled in and headed for the bright lights of Singapore City.

The bars in downtown Singapore were smarter and more expensive than in most of the other Far Eastern watering holes, which was another of the improvements introduced by Mr Lee Kwan Yu. Most of the nightclubs and bars were in fact set in the new high rise hotels, provided Western-style food and demure floor shows suitable for family entertainment. Prostitution and drug dealing – what there was of it – had been driven heavily underground and the whole place emanated clean living.

The one exception to this was Bhugis Street (pronounced Boogie Street). This was the gathering place of the Kai-Tais – local transvestites. These were handsome, slim young men who turned up in Bhugis Street each evening clutching bundles under their arms before disappearing into the public lavatories and emerging a short time later as glamorous and curvy women in stylish long evening dresses, to stroll around among the rough wooden tables flaunting themselves in front of the gathering of sailors out looking for an evening of fun, amusement and booze. Like us, most of the visiting men present had arrived in groups, there being safety in numbers and for the most part they simply sat drinking and passing lewd remarks towards the patrolling kai-tais, which would usually generate a coquettish response.

As the evening wore on one or more of the kai-tais would insert themselves among a group around a table, giggling and simpering as they did so. In the light of the gas and oil lamps they could look extraordinarily attractive especially when they were far enough away across the table for the five o'clock shadow to disappear behind the make-up and dim lighting. Booze tended to befuddle minds and occasionally a sailor would wander off with a kai-tai, thinking he had found the love of his life despite the loud imprecations of his friends. I heard of more than one story of a mariner who had woken up with the worst shock of his life and had suffered the further ignominy of becoming a rather obvious patient at the sick bay. We didn't lose anyone that evening and when stomachs began to feel the need of solids we all trooped off in the direction of Fatty's, the other half of the Bhugis Street experience. Fatty's was a peculiar kind of restaurant; the inside part nestled under a sprawling ramshackle old colonial building while the rest, the bulk of the restaurant, spread outside up and down the pavement and far out into the adjacent road with a sea of rough wooden tables and chairs all sheltering under big parasols and canopies.

Service was instant and attentive. Each arrival was personally seated by 'Fatty', a huge fat Chinaman with a beaming gap-toothed smile, clad in an off-white singlet and khaki 'Empire Building' shorts. He would bustle about settling everyone exactly where he wanted them and would conclude the exercise with his announcement of the menu. "You wan' meat or you wan' fish?" he would boom. The answer required only one word whereupon he was gone in a flash never to be seen again that evening unless one passed him on the way out. I never had a bad meal at Fatty's. I rarely knew precisely what I was eating but whatever it was it was always superb.

Our run ashore broke up into smaller groups as the evening wore on and we all rolled happily northward towards the dockyard in a variety of transport as the night turned to early morning.

Despite the best intentions of the revellers, quite a few of us were distracted on the way home by the wonderful smells emerging from the tiny wayside cooking stalls. Even after a sumptuous feast at Fatty's, it was commonplace to end the evening – or start the morning – sitting on plain wooden benches or rickety folding chairs over bowls of unidentified Malay or Chinese food on the edge of a monsoon ditch, accompanied by cold Tiger beer, all for the price of a few Singapore dollars. We called all of these family-run establishments after a famous hotel chain. Thus, there was the Nee Soon Hilton, the Sembawang Hilton, the Seletar Hilton and so forth.

Singapore in those days was in many respects a model modern state. Everything was spotlessly clean, the government was moving rapidly to build and develop infrastructure, commerce and business whilst maintaining a strong economy with no debts. The drug threat was under firm control and the people seemed to be uniquely honest. I had personal experience of this a few years later when staying with my wife in married quarters near *HMS Terror*, the naval base adjacent to Sembawang dockyard.

We had set out on a shopping trip down into the city and had determined to go in by bus. We strolled down to the bus stop and waited, sitting on the bench conveniently sheltered from the sun. Unusually, nobody joined us in the wait for the bus, which took some time to arrive. We waited, chatting about what we hoped to buy and where, enjoying the cooling breeze and the shade, while taking in the peculiar and distinctive jungle smell that surrounded us. When the bus duly arrived we climbed happily aboard, leaving my wife's handbag sitting, all alone on the bench beside the bus stop. We had reached the outskirts of the City before the handbag was found to be missing. In a panic we hopped off the bus at the next stop, dodged across the road and lined up at the north-going bus stop. We waited in tense silence for nearly ten minutes before Irene blurted out that the handbag contained her passport, purse, local currency and air ticket back to England. The bus arrived, very full, so we had to stand most of the way. The journey seemed to drag out much longer than the one we had just taken in the opposite direction but eventually we reached the Sembawang stop and squeezed past the latest batch of standing passengers to get off. We waited for the bus to pull away and as it did so I looked across the road to the other stop and there, sitting where it had been left was my wife's errant handbag. She ran across the road, threading through the light traffic and pounced on the handbag. I crossed the road more slowly, sat on the bench and waited while she rummaged through the fairly full bag. When she looked up her face was one big smile. Neither the handbag nor its contents had been touched. Such was Singapore.

Like most places around the waterfronts of the world, Singapore could offer a less attractive side. One such experience was known to occur when late night revellers were weaving their way through the silent dockyard, returning to their ships. The dockyard was usually quiet and very dark at night. The only human occupants of the yard tended to be the guards on the gates and an occasional security patrol. There were rats, and feral cats but most unnerving were the packs of pi-dogs. These animals looked a bit like scrawny dingoes but came in a range of sizes and colours – mostly shades of brown. They lurked generally unseen during daytime, in the shadowy unused parts of the yard but at night they were in the habit of emerging to stalk lonely sailors walking – perhaps unsteadily – back to their floating homes. Usually a glance behind would identify a single dog slinking noiselessly along, following at about twenty yards. A few minutes later there would be two of them, then three, a little closer. If they remained undisturbed they would grow bolder and closer and before long a pack of about twenty or so would be trailing the unfortunate single mariner. I never heard, myself, of anyone being savaged by these dogs but the experience of being trailed by them was not nice.

Chapter 18

Homeward Bound

We left Singapore looking a little cleaner, a little smarter and probably riding somewhat lower in the water, having embarked several tons of suits, shirts, china, silks, dresses, pewter, radios and other electrical gadgets as well as a full load of fuel for the ship and her aircraft. Efforts to repair the burnt-out air conditioning system had been unsuccessful so we all continued to sweat below decks.

Singapore seemed to have been a morale booster for the boys in the squadrons, partly because the programme of repairs had put an end, at least temporarily, to the usual shipboard spit and polish as well as the other irritating forms of bullshit often imposed from above in big ships. The free-ranging opportunities to run ashore and use the very favourable rate of exchange to stock up on 'rabbits' and exotic booze in equal measure had also helped quite a bit to raise spirits. It was a carefree and happy ship's company that waved goodbye to Singapore and contemplated arrival home into the arms of loved ones in only ten days or so.

As the ship steamed south past Sumatra and Java towards the Gulf of Carpentaria and Thursday Island at the northern tip of Cape York, the atmosphere on board became more relaxed. Very little flying was taking place and most of the squadron maintenance effort was concentrated on ensuring that the aircraft were in a fit state to disembark. The flight deck became a recreational area except when aircraft were dragged up on deck for tethered engine runs and other tasks which could not take place in the hangar.

The wardroom mess quickly became busier and although the two-hour limit on the 'beer issues' was strictly enforced, the after dinner social gatherings frequently ran on late into the night. It seemed as though we were getting in practice for letting our hair down in preparation for the Christmas celebrations which would begin a few weeks after the ship's arrival in Sydney.

As we passed down the east coast outside the Great Barrier Reef, I was introduced to a peculiarly Australian system for passing the ship's company through customs which I thought was far superior to the aggressive and unhelpful system frequently experienced by warships and sailors returning home to Britain.

I took off as part of a three aircraft section to fly into Coffs Harbour and pick up a large team of Australian customs officers. The aircrews were under strict instructions regarding the return trip to the fleet offshore, which was heading slowly south. Two aircraft could easily have accommodated the customs team but three were programmed so that all of the passengers had the opportunity to see outside the aircraft and take in the fantastic scenery of the shoreline and the Barrier Reef as we returned to the aircraft carrier. The direct route between Coffs Harbour and the ship should have taken about twenty minutes but our scenic tour lasted over an hour, with our passengers snapping away with their cameras as we passed close over the sights. When we arrived back at the fleet, the aircraft split up with the other two winching some of their passengers down to the escorts while I continued to land my team on board *Melbourne*. As I shut down the engine and the passengers were helped out I saw that they were being treated to a VIP reception team including the rarely seen Admiral himself, the Commander and several other worthies. They were whisked off among smiles and handshakes to what was probably a sumptuous lunch in the Admiral's day cabin. "More than I ever got," I reflected to no one in particular.

The last few days of the voyage down the coast to Sydney had turned into something of a holiday cruise. We entertained the customs team in the wardroom then they went off to try the hospitality of the Chiefs' Mess, then the Petty Officers'. Dinner each evening was a sumptuous affair with decent Australian and French wines followed with short speeches afterwards, when the port decanters circulated several times. During the day, helicopters took off in ones and twos, ostensibly to transfer important bits of kit to one or other of the escorts but always carrying a couple of customs officers and their cameras.

Two days before the squadrons were due to fly off and the ship to enter the vast expanse of Sydney Harbour, it was payback time for our friendly customs team. It was time for the whole ship's company to go through customs and since we would be flying off some hours before the ship entered harbour, the aircrew were processed first. We were all issued with customs declaration forms and as every item to be imported into Australia had to be entered separately, most of us, including me, needed several forms. The customs desk was set up in one of the briefing rooms and aircrew were called forward by squadron and alphabetically. A queue formed in the passageway outside and when my turn came I marched in clutching my small sheaf of forms. I was invited to sit at a desk opposite the examining customs officer. Curiously, another of the customs officers was seated on my side of the desk, looking rather like the 'friend of the accused' – and that was in effect what he turned out to be.

The examining customs officer peered carefully at each of my completed declaration forms. His lips pursed, he turned back to the first form, made a couple of pencil marks in the margin and examined the remainder of the form, looking grim. The man on my side gave me a nod and an encouraging grin. I have always had a problem of unreasonable and unnecessary nervousness when faced with often grim customs inspections and my experience of British customs officers was that most of them had not been issued with any sense of humour at all, leading on to the thought that their parents had never married. My attempt to respond to the encouraging smile from my side of the table had turned into a sort of fixed rictus grin.

"I see you have five watches," the interrogator challenged from the other side of the table.

"Er, yes," I started to reply.

"Let me see that," said the friend of the accused. The paper was handed over, and examined on my side of the table. "Yes, I see," he continued slowly, then, more brightly, "Yeah, well there it is. Do you swim?" This was addressed to me. I nodded. My throat had dried sufficiently to prevent speech.

"Well, that's OK then," continued the one who I was beginning to think of as 'the nice man'. Turning to his colleague, he launched into an explanation which went something along the lines of "He needs one for flying, one for swimming, one for normal wear, one for formal evening wear and one which he is entitled to bring in as a gift." He looked across the table and with the ghost of a smile his colleague placed a big flourishing red tick on the form. Several other questions followed in similar vein but before I had the chance to frame a reply they were each swept up in the same style as the first one and batted straight back. Eventually we all stood up, shook hands and bade each other "G'day". As I strode happily back to my cabin with my red-ticked forms and clearance stamp I couldn't help contrasting the pleasant experience I had just undergone with another customs clearance, on the far side of the world in Panama. On that occasion I was not attempting to get my own things through customs, I was instead trying to prise some packages out of the customs office which contained essential spares for a ship's flight helicopter. Standing by the desk in the crowded, humid customs office in the passenger terminal of Panama City airport, I could see my packages on a table running the length of the far side of the room but as I stood, sweating and frustrated, the hairy Zapata-moustached individual in a grubby sweat-stained khaki tunic surmounted by a 'Sam Browne' belt pretended that he could not understand what I wanted, then he could not understand me, then he couldn't see the packages. Eventually we stood on either side of the desk with the four small but vital packages on the counter between us as the toad on the other side started to talk of duty to be paid and 'impounding'. This difficulty had in fact been anticipated by my elders and betters in the ship and I had been issued with a bundle of 'slush money' in small denomination American dollars. After more than an hour of frustration and argument I was finally able to return to the ship with the packages but with my bundle of dollars significantly depleted.

I mused that British customs stood somewhere between these two extremes as I started my packing for home.

****

The day of final departure from the carrier dawned bright and clear with a light breeze from the shoreline now crisply visible a few miles away to starboard. I was to be tail-end Charlie in the formation of eight – always assuming all the aircraft remained serviceable at take-off. We were the last squadron to leave the ship, having provided a planeguard helicopter while the jets launched, followed by the six Trackers. Each squadron had drawn away astern of the ship before forming up into tight smart formation and running in low and stylishly up the port side, giving the ship a farewell flypast. It is always more difficult to make a helicopter formation look good, but I could see from the back of the double echelon that the boys were on form. We swept up the port side just above deck level like a pack of enthusiastic hunting dogs heading for the kennel. As well as the crew of four, every space in every aircraft was packed to capacity with kit and 'rabbits'. Mine was no exception. The cabin door had to remain shut to stop the booty from falling out.

We opened up the formation as we flew round to the seaward side of Kingsford Smith International and remained just offshore until we reached the southern suburbs of Sydney where we settled down to follow the familiar coastline down past the steel town of Wollongong, on past Kiama before the shape of the town of Nowra, nestling on the banks of the Shoalhaven River came into view. A word from the lead aircraft and the formation tightened up to look pretty as we flew over the town that had been my home for two years. Minutes later we were flying low, fast and neat, at two hundred feet, down the main runway of the air station, before executing a very smooth 'NATO Break' to allow each aircraft in turn to swing round in a constant three hundred and sixty degree turn on to 'Finals' and then run in to land. The column of big white and blue helicopters then taxied one by one into the home dispersal to line up in front of the cheering, happy throng of families and friends waiting to greet us. It was enough to bring a tear to the eye of even the saltiest sailor.

As soon as all of the helicopters were lined up, the engines were cut simultaneously and the slick exercise of returning home ended as impressively as it had begun. On the end of the line I saw my wife Irene, looking radiant and waving. As I climbed down from the cockpit I caught sight of a small flurry of movement from the welcoming group as my little two-year-old daughter broke ranks and ran as fast as she could towards the aircraft. The cabin door slid open and Fred the observer eased himself out from around the pile of goodies. At that point, Rebecca, my daughter, reached up and dragged out from the front of the heap of cargo a tiny, toddler-sized wickerwork armchair. She plonked it on the hot tarmac and promptly sat in it. At this point I also noticed a thin, grim looking Australian customs officer bearing down on the scene. Clearly nobody had told him that we had already cleared customs. Nevertheless he was headed determinedly towards the little girl sitting in the chair. By the time I had hauled myself out of the cockpit and around to the side of the aircraft a battle of wills had begun and was now in full spate, watched by the remainder of my crew. The customs officer reckoned that the chair was made of wickerwork and therefore not allowed into Australia. Rebecca cared not a hoot for that and she hung on grimly to the arms of the chair, producing a huge angry squawk at every attempt by officialdom to dispossess her of her new present from Daddy. I attempted to reason with the stubborn young man but he was not open to persuasion, not from me at any rate. I showed him the necessary certificate of 'bug-freeness' and explained that the chair was only temporarily imported into Australia because we were leaving soon for England and the chair would be departing with the rest my family goods and chattels. He was still not to be moved. But he had a bigger problem with the little girl who was in firm possession of the chair and was clearly a believer that 'possession was nine tenths of the law'. Every attempt to wrest the chair away from Rebecca was met with massive, determined and noisy protest.

The chair has been with my family for forty years now and is shared these days by my twin three-year-old granddaughters.

As soon as possible after we had greeted each other Irene drove over to the wardroom to wait while I signed the essential aircraft documents and then helped to unload all the kit and presents from the aircraft cabin into several trolleys which, with the remainder of the crew, we wheeled across to the squadron huts. I located my locker in the dusty changing room and changed quickly from flying overalls into my tropical uniform. As I emerged from the squadron hut the big 'Golden Holden' station wagon purred into the parking area, driven by Irene with Rebecca waving from her seat in the back. She had her new wickerwork armchair snuggled close in beside her and was gripping it firmly with one tiny white-knuckled hand.

In ten minutes I had crammed every remaining space in the huge vehicle and with my fresh but now sweaty shirt sticking to my back I climbed in beside Irene to be chauffeured off to our home. The drive took less than ten minutes with conversation muted by the excited and incomprehensible chatter coming from the back seat.

As we cruised slowly along Berry Street I could see, looking ahead, a familiar form shimmering out of the heat haze. Spoofy our temporarily adopted big black Labrador, had assumed his 'welcome home' position. He was sitting, bolt upright, like a sentry posted alongside the nearest gate post. As we approached the turn into the driveway he remained stock still, apart from the giveaway of his tail briskly sweeping the dust behind him from side to side. Even through the heat haze I could see that his gaze was riveted on the approaching car. We pulled slowly into the drive and Irene drove carefully down towards the house as each car window in succession seemed to be filled by the joyous leaping form of a black Labrador. I knew that as soon as I tried to get out of the car I would be covered in dog slobber – and I was not disappointed.

Chapter 19

Tragedy Again

The local press had been out in force at the Air Station to record the homecoming of the *Melbourne* Air Group. Nowra was a small town and the rest of the world was often regarded as far away and unimportant. This was sometimes reflected in the local newspaper with banner headlines announcing such underwhelming news as 'MR AND MRS JONES LEAVE FOR HOLIDAY IN UK'. In relation to this, the arrival in force, of twenty-one naval aircraft returning from an absence of several months defending the interests of Australia in the 'Near north' with fifty-eight airborne warriors all arriving at once, to be followed by ground parties the next day with another three hundred or so men was very big news indeed. More than half of the Air Group had homes in or around Nowra so about two thousand people representing families and friends would be directly affected. Add the effect on local businesses, and entertainment centres and the arrival home of the Air Group could be considered the event of the year.

Reporters and photographers were scampering around the various squadron dispersals interviewing officers and men as well as arranging suitably posed photographs which would dominate the next day's edition of the paper. The press always seem to go for the slightly different and more glamorous subjects when they are setting out a celebratory spread like this one. They believe that pilots rate higher than other aircrew and fixed-wing aircraft of all types are more interesting than lowly helicopters. Accordingly the main press activity was concentrated over on the dispersal areas of the two fixed-wing squadrons while for the most part we helicopter crews were undisturbed, allowing me to complete my work, get the car packed and head off home fairly quickly. Another form of special attraction for the press men was anything unusual. In this respect they looked for wives with new babies, recently promoted husbands or aircrew who were unusual – or foreign to Australia. I was not really within this category as it was widely considered that Brits could not really be included in the special interest category. Americans, however, were very definitely considered 'special interest'.

Jerry was American. He had been recently promoted and he was a pilot, albeit a pilot of the rather slower and less exciting Tracker Squadron. He had a charming and attractive young wife as well as a couple of small children. He was the reporters delight. He was a photographers' 'Manna from Heaven'.

Several reporters hovered around Jerry and his family asking the usually predictable and somewhat inane questions, while photographers darted about, interrupting the interviews and attempting to move their subjects here and there.

One of the photographs of Jerry being greeted by his family would dominate the front page of the next morning's paper, with the interview with Jerry leading the report underneath the photograph.

****

When *Melbourne* docked in Sydney later that afternoon, Jerry learnt that his plan for the transport of his new Honda motorbike had gone awry. He had arranged for the big bike to be loaded onto one of the Navy lorries picking up the stores and spares due to be transported by road to Nowra. By early evening the lorries had been loaded ready for departure the following morning, but despite several attempts, there was no room for the motorbike. It was just too big.

When Jerry received the telephone call from the officer in charge of the ground party to tell him that his bike had been landed from the ship and secured as safely as possible on the jetty but that it would be left there, he was faced with an unwanted dilemma.

The valuable motorbike could not be left on the jetty but it was not yet insured for use in Australia so even if he could locate someone to ride the bike down to Nowra, Jerry could not bring himself to suggest to anyone else that they should ride the uninsured vehicle over the one hundred miles separating Sydney from Nowra.

Jerry held an American driving licence as well as an Australian one. He had no idea whether his Australian license covered motorbikes but he was pretty sure his American one did. This led him to a plan to resolve his problem. In a quick phone call he managed to set up an expensive one-day insurance deal before setting off for Sydney. He cadged a lift on one of the lorries returning to the Garden Island Dockyard on the following morning and made his way through the dockyard towards the jetty where *Melbourne* was moored. He was anxious to put his plan into effect and had no reason to go on board so he checked the big Honda over, swung himself into the comfortable saddle, pressed the electric starter and, very tentatively, set off towards the dockyard gate.

Jerry had only ever ridden his motorbike for a circuit of a few yards along the jetty in Yokosuka and again, briefly, in Singapore. He had never exceeded a speed of fifteen miles an hour and had probably rarely, if ever, changed out of first gear. It was a big, powerful, heavy bike and most definitely not recommended for novice riders.

Jerry rode the bike away from the dockyard and south through the Sydney suburbs, ignoring the shop and van signs in Greek and then Serbo-Croat as he passed through Little Greece and Little Yugoslavia. He tried to keep away from the main roads consequently taking rather longer than he had imagined, to thread his way through the congested and cluttered side streets. Gradually he became a little more confident and when the conditions allowed, he began, tentatively, to increase speed. By the time he left the shop lined streets and had started to pass through residential districts he was able to maintain a steady thirty to forty miles per hour. This was OK provided that the other traffic was moving at the same pace but as soon as the road cleared ahead of his bike, the traffic building up behind him began to press him and eventually the queue leader would pull out and whoosh past him. Cars were not too bad but box vans and huge articulated trucks caused such a buffet of air that Jerry wobbled alarmingly on his bike. At one stage he became so nervous that he pulled off into a dirt covered lay-by on the left of the highway.

Jerry stopped the bike, heaved it up on to its stand and wandered away to take a break and calm down. He decided that he would need to speed up a bit to match the general traffic speed. Having made up his mind he climbed back on the bike, started it up and stared back down the road, searching for a long break in the traffic. Six or seven minutes later the road from Sydney cleared sufficiently for Jerry to swing the bike uncertainly out onto the Princes Highway and turn it in the direction of Nowra.

With a clear road, Jerry picked up speed so he was able to keep ahead of any unseen traffic and as he did so his confidence grew. He had passed Wollongong which with the picturesque Kembla State Forest on his right gave him just under thirty miles to go. By this stage he had brought the bike up to just below the fifty miles per hour state-wide speed limit and had thereby evaded most of the pressure from faster vehicles coming up behind him.

The road began to descend and climb and then to weave around rock formations and stands of trees. Jerry's initial nervousness had dissipated and he now felt more confident with the big machine. He swept down a steeply descending stretch of road which eased into a shallow left-hand bend at the bottom of the slope. Too late, he realised that the deceptively shallow bend was tightening up as it continued. Big heavy motorbikes require a particular technique in negotiating steep bends – and Jerry did not know what that technique was. He tried to heave the bike around to follow the steepening bend but the momentum it had acquired was too much and instead of following the road, the bike fell onto its side, still travelling at nearly fifty miles per hour. The bike now lying on its side but with Jerry still aboard, swept across the road, through the flimsy fence before it slammed into a vertical rock wall. Jerry died instantly.

At about the same time the homecoming issue of the Nowra paper was circulating through the town with Jerry's smiling face dominating the front page.

Chapter 20

The Boys Are Back

The Air Station was fairly quiet. Many people were away on post-deployment leave and there was very little flying taking place in the front-line squadrons. Christmas was less than a month away and my family was already coming to terms with the planning and arrangements necessary to prepare for our departure from Australia only two months after Christmas. We intended to use the leave I was due to make one more expedition around the south-east of Australia. In the meantime I had little to do at work except carry out the occasional duty of Duty Commanding Officer. This seemed to come round frequently and in the early days after the Air Group had returned, the duty session seemed to be regularly spiced up by the results of some social gathering on or off the base.

It was only after I had agreed to do yet another Friday duty that I realised there was a big party planned at the Golf Club on the other side of the river. Actually I wasn't too fussed. I wasn't a member of the Golf Club so I wasn't likely to receive an invitation.

The evening was quiet to the level of boredom. The only subject of conversation over dinner in the mess seemed to be the new set of curtains, or 'drapes', as they seemed to be called, which decorated the wide floor to ceiling French windows at the far end of the anteroom. The windows opened onto a pleasant little lawn where a barbecue was often set up. Previously, the windows had been fringed with an elderly group of discoloured rags which could not be drawn closed for fear that they would actually disintegrate. The replacement curtains could not have been in place for more than three months but they were already looking distinctly sad. I commented on the wavy line running horizontally along the curtains midway between top and bottom, dividing the quite presentable top half from a heavily stained bottom half.

After a few polite but abortive attempts to change the subject I was treated to an unexpurgated version of the whole grisly tale. The damaged curtains, I was told, represented a small revolt against the Mess Committee. At the time when I was serving as Senior Pilot of the Operational Flying Training Squadron nobody seemed to want anything to do with the Mess Committee but when the front line squadrons had left for their deployment on board *Melbourne* there had been a resurgence of interest in the wardroom mess and its committee. Several of the younger officers, including a couple of 'Pommies' on loan, had set out to make the mess more comfortable and to hide some of the less endearing traits of an ancient wooden hut. Their group leader within the committee was another loan officer – a very 'proper' young man who had about him the air of a young British aristocrat. Allegedly at his prompting a decision had been made to spend some of the considerable mess funds in acquiring some decent curtains and some better rugs for the floor than the three feet by two Navy-issue ones that were presently scattered about. A small group of two members of the Mess Committee had been delegated to travel up to Sydney to one of the smarter stores and select the required goods. Typically, after the new curtains were hung, some of the residents of the mess began to take exception to them. They became a subject for fierce booze-fuelled debate and as time passed, attitudes hardened. The curtains were described as 'Poofy' and given other even ruder epithets. Eventually, towards the end of a particularly volatile 'Happy Hour' half a dozen inebriated malcontents had lined up and piddled on the drawn curtains to 'make them look more lived in'. Thankfully, the officer who had put so much effort into trying to improve the ambience of the mess had by then already left to return to Britain.

Attempts had been made to clean the curtains but, sadly, this had only resulted in achieving the present unfortunate state. My dinner companions were phlegmatic about the whole incident. They compared it with previous japes such as driving a road roller through the front and out of the back of the building leaving the structure near collapse or riding a motorcycle through the unopened windows. It was called 'letting off steam'.

I finished my dinner, pondered on what I had heard, felt glad that I hadn't been anywhere nearby when the desecration occurred and settled down to read a book. Later I drifted around the airfield on my 'rounds' before waiting for the bar to close and then headed off to bed in the 'duty' cabin, mentally offering grateful thanks for a quiet evening.

At about half past midnight, the telephone beside the bed jangled me into wakefulness. The bedside light was still on and I still had my book gripped firmly in my hands, in which position I had fallen asleep while trying to read it.

"DCO sir?" asked the disembodied voice into my ear.

"Yes," I said.

"This is Chief of the Watch in the guardroom sir. We've got the police here sir."

"What's the problem?"

"It's a couple of officers sir. They want to speak to you."

"Who?" I asked. "The officers or the police?"

There was a pause. "Well, both really sir," said the duty chief slowly, "but I think it would be better to talk to the police first."

"Right, give me five minutes," I said, climbing reluctantly out of the hard narrow bed.

"I'll give them a coffee, sir." He rang off. I wondered who was being offered the coffee. 'Probably the police,' I thought, 'but the airborne warriors with them were more likely to need it!'

I dressed as quickly as I could in blue trousers and white tropical shirt, known as Red Sea Rig in Britain, locked the cabin and went outside to where the official car was parked. Two minutes later and seven minutes after the phone call I was shaking hands with two tired-looking policemen as the Duty Chief introduced them. I took the only empty chair around the table, nodded thanks to the Chief as a mug of steaming coffee was placed in front of me and looked enquiringly towards the policemen.

They were pretty good about what they had to say to me. They were, as they put it, not wishing to come down heavily on young officers who had just returned from overseas but they were pretty pissed off at some of the behaviour they had to put up with.

They had been cruising around and through Nowra in a standard Friday late night patrol when their attention had been caught by an elderly Ford Falcon proceeding slowly but erratically through the town. They had followed the Ford through the town and out along the road to the airfield in their patrol car. About a mile short of the Air Station the progress of the Ford became so erratic and disjointed that it appeared likely to crash into the roadside ditch. The policemen switched on their blue lights, flicked the siren on and off and pulled around in front of their quarry.

The Ford had two occupants. Ernie, and his Tracker Squadron friend Frank, both returning from the Golf Club party. For some reason they had decided that Frank should dress up as a city toff and Ernie should go along in drag – in this case a fetching bright green taffeta dress complete with handbag and high-heeled shoes. The Golf Club party was not a fancy dress party but this hadn't seemed to register with the pair, nor had it dented their effervescent enthusiasm during the course of the evening.

Frank, sitting behind the wheel, had wound down the window. "Wassa madder?" he had enquired mildly.

"Step out of the car please sir," said the officer in typical cop manner. Frank was not really in an appropriate state to step out of anything so he responded with the first thing that came into his head.

"Aw, Fuggoff," he said.

The night was dark and moonless and with no lights other than the car headlights, neither of the police officers had noticed that the heavily made up chunky woman in the left-hand seat was not quite what she appeared to be.

"Watch yer language in front of the lady," said the cop. The 'lady' had completely forgotten that he was attired in green taffeta with handbag and high heels to match. He heard part of what the policeman had said, assumed it was an intended slight on his manhood and with the sudden burst of energy that only the very drunk seem to be able to come up with from time to time, he threw open the left-hand door, knocking off balance the other policeman, who had come round to that side of the car. Ernie had leapt out of the car and, in a flurry of green taffeta, swung a haymaking right hook at the police officer catching him a glancing blow on the chin.

"Who are you callin' a fuckin' lady, ya poofta!" bellowed Ernie as the other policeman kicked his nyloned legs from under him and deftly snapped on a pair of handcuffs.

Frank couldn't get out of the car on his own so he was helped out and bundled, none too gently into the segregated back of the police car. The police driver switched off the lights and engine of the Ford, slammed the doors and took his own car around in an impressive U-turn back down the road towards Nowra.

The two miscreants were now ruefully sobering up in the 'tank' at the back of the Nowra police station.

"Oh dear," I said. Then after a pause to gather my thoughts, "We would like them back as soon as possible, of course."

"It's tricky," said the number two cop. "He took a swing at me," he fingered his jaw as he said this.

"Didn't you say he was carrying a handbag?" I asked, innocently.

The Chief joined the conversation. "Wouldn't look too good if it got about that a drunk in a dress knocked you down."

The other cop said, "Nope." A ghost of a smile passed and was gone. We continued talking around the situation until just after two o'clock when it was agreed that the pair should have sobered up sufficiently to be passed into naval custody. By this time we had discovered that both of the policemen were ex-Navy which explained why our two tearaways looked like getting such a decent break.

Twenty minutes or so later I left the guardroom and went back to bed, having handed over the problem to the Officer of the Day who would greet the returning pair and arrange an interview with the Station Commander.

****

I had another interesting duty a week or so later. This followed some sort of parade – not the full Air Station 'Divisions' – which had in turn provided the reason for another 'Happy Hour'. Happy hours were always likely to cause problems for duty officers, who were expected to maintain reasonable decorum in the mess and to shut the bar at the end of the evening or when he judged it necessary to do so.

The Happy Hour had ended formally at seven in the evening but the party was still going – no longer strong, but definitely still going – when I drifted in to see that all was well. The first object I saw was a sub-lieutenant in a slightly grubby white formal tropical uniform – known universally and for obvious reasons as an 'Ice Cream Suit'. He was lying horizontally alongside the foot rail in front of the bar, moving, but only just.

"He's drunk," I announced to no one in particular, as I approached the bar.

"Nah, nah, nah, sir," responded the barman. "Look," he said. "Ya can see he's not drunk – he's still holding his beer upright." Indeed he was. I withdrew temporarily to allow the other revellers the opportunity to resolve the problem.

I was allocated only one more turn as Duty Commanding Officer before I finally packed my kit and headed back to the northern Hemisphere. That was on New Year's Eve – December 31st 1972. The wardroom was letting its hair down but many of the younger and more volatile individuals were far away on seasonal leave so the party was fun but not so wild as some of the others I had experienced. We had a small but amusing incident when two of the few remaining sub-lieutenants got themselves very drunk and decided that they would test the strength of a regulation issue aircrew watch. The party was only in its early hours when they staggered outside, still arguing incomprehensibly and stumbled into the adjacent car park. The watch tester lay down with his arm and the watch stretched out under one of the back wheels of a sporty Holden Monaro while his companion was attempting to get behind the wheel to drive the car backwards and thus test the strength of the watch. Fortunately, the plan failed dismally. The 'driver' didn't have any keys to start the vehicle and while searching his pockets he fell out of the car, bumped his head and was found propped against the side of the Monaro, quietly sleeping off the effects of the booze. His companion, once he had achieved the semi-vertical position, also fell asleep and was found still lying behind the car, one arm still stretched out on the ground behind a rear wheel.

I was temporarily diverted from the festivities while the two revellers were helped off to bed by their friends.

The party rolled on through the evening until I detached myself just before midnight and went with Irene across to the 'quarterdeck' in front of the Captain's office where the Station flagstaff was located, with the 'ship's bell' alongside it. There we were met by the Quartermaster of the Watch who was accompanied by the youngest man on the base. As the clocks began to chime the midnight hour we commenced the age old naval tradition of ringing in the New Year with 'sixteen bells' – twice the normal 'eight bells' which usually marked the fourth hour of the watch. It was said that this was eight bells to bid the old year farewell and a further eight to welcome the new.

It was a strangely moving little ceremony as the small group stood beside the young sailor who solemnly and steadily rang the 'ship's bell' to the count of the Quartermaster. As the last reverberation of the bell died away, both sailors turned smartly towards me, saluted and said, "Happy New Year, sir." I returned the salute and the greeting and it was over. I looked towards Irene who had a single tear running down her cheek.

My duty did not require me to remain overnight but I stayed until the party was over and the bar closed before wearily strolling off to the car park and driving slowly back between the forests of tall gum trees, black in the darkness, towards the house in Berry Street. Halfway along the road Irene said, rather suddenly, "What about the Mosses?" Mr and Mrs Moss were an elderly Scottish couple who we had met briefly a few weeks beforehand. They had emigrated to Australia some years ago and they seemed rather lost and lonely with no close family and few friends living locally. In our brief meeting it had been clear to both of us that in their advancing years they had grown very homesick for Scotland particularly as the New Year approached. There would be celebrations, they agreed, but not on the scale of their youth in Aberdeenshire. They couldn't really come to terms with a New Year in temperatures of one hundred degrees Fahrenheit with no bitter cold wind to keep the parties going indoors sustained by skirling pipes, dancing, whisky and peat fires – and there was no snow on the ground. In an unthinking moment we had promised that we would 'First Foot' them after midnight on New Year's Eve. That was the promise that Irene now raised as we motored down the lonely road towards home, to a big black welcoming dog – and uninterrupted sleep.

"You can't go knocking on the door at this hour, it's nearly four in the morning," I said, firmly, I thought.

"We said we would, and we should," said Irene, equally firmly.

"We can't. It's uncivilised."

"It's New Year's Eve and we promised."

"No. It's unfair." As we neared the edge of the town I could sense in the darkness inside the car that my control of the situation was already slipping.

"We'll just drive past and see if there are any lights on," said Irene. I thought that was a reasonable compromise and so decided not to raise the issue of Spoofy being left even longer on his own. To reach the Moss's one-storey house we had to drive on down Berry Street past our own house. I had silently gathered another argument about how unfair it was to leave the dog for even longer than we already had when the headlights picked up a familiar shape loping along the pavement. Our lodger dog had been out once again on one of his late night prowls and was now heading happily home clutching some indistinguishable trophy between his strong jaws. Irene had seen him as well so there was no longer any point in deploying my as yet unspoken argument. We drove on towards the Moss's home.

I cruised slowly along the road where every house, including our destination, was in complete darkness. As I eased the car into the kerbside, Irene already had the door open. I put a restraining hand on her arm. "Look," I said, "the place is in complete darkness. They've gone to bed."

She was undeterred. "I'll just go and knock gently, once, on the door," she said over her shoulder as she advanced across the grass strip separating the kerb from the pavement.

"OK Once," I responded, resignedly.

Irene didn't knock. She pressed the door bell. As if a massive master switch had been thrown, the whole house exploded into light and activity. Within moments the door was opened wide and both Mr and Mrs Moss were exchanging enthusiastic New Year greetings with my wife. I parked the car and gave up any thought of sleep that night. I had wondered at Irene's foresight in arranging for our baby-sitter to stay overnight but now I realised the scale of her contingency planning. We were welcomed like long lost cousins. We opened all the doors, carried coal in through them, drank quite a few drams of whisky and even indulged in a bit of amateur Scottish dancing. As our hosts were still fully clothed and well prepared for entertaining, we would have been a big disappointment had we failed to turn up. That evening an Irish lady and her Sassenach husband brought a little bit of Scotland to two Caledonian émigrés far from home in south-eastern Australia.

We arrived back at our own home several hours later to find both our daughter and her baby-sitter still asleep but their guardian dog sitting wearing his slightly affronted "where have you been and where's my breakfast?" look. If he had been able to wear one he would have been glancing meaningfully at the watch on his wrist/paw.

Chapter 21

Going Home

It seemed to me that the flying and working activity level around the squadron and to some extent around the Air Station, as we all returned from the Christmas and New Year holiday break, was a bit like that prevailing when the British Expeditionary Force arrived in France in1940. Almost nothing was happening. And whatever did happen was taking place very slowly. The younger officers in the squadron were bored and several of them found an unusual way to ease the boredom. They started building their own single-seat aeroplanes. These were not models or toys; they were supposed to be the real thing. Some American companies had started off the hobby of home aircraft assembly a few years before and it had now caught on in quite a big way. At first the builders worked single-handed but friends soon became interested and small construction teams began to emerge. Work at weekends and in the evening increased the production rate and soon there were sounds of engines being fired up and the first sight came of a small aircraft taxiing under its own power. I wondered how the builders would cope with airworthiness certificates and other official requirements, but thought it better not to ask.

One slightly more senior officer from the Carrier Air Group found time hanging heavily on his hands. This was the Carrier Borne Ground Liaison Officer, an army officer attached to every aircraft carrier whose job it was to organise shore bombardment and strike sorties and occasionally to act as Forward Air Controller, reporting fall of shot in the case of gunnery actions and the accuracy of bombs in air attacks. He had a small team of a sergeant and two soldiers to help him run his section. In harbour, when the ship was undergoing 'Self Maintenance' there was little or nothing for any of these men to do so they tended to base themselves in the more spacious accommodation offered by the Naval Air Station. Unfortunately, there wasn't much for them to do there either, so the officer in charge, a major of artillery, fell to hanging around the aircraft builders, then to helping them, and finally to starting his own light aircraft construction project. Such seaborne army officers were invariably given an irreverent title within the Air Group. The acronym describing their job – CBGLO – is twisted to become 'Seaballs' a title to which they all happily respond.

Our 'Seaballs' was an effervescent character trying to be friend and confidant to everybody whilst displaying the earnest enthusiasm of a fourteen-year-old boy towards every task and project that could come his way. Because of this and his sometimes amusing antics, the sub-lieutenants dubbed him 'Major Laugh' (because he "Made yer laugh" I was told) but they worked diligently alongside him when he became an aircraft builder.

The first homemade aircraft to emerge for a test run at speed down the runway one Saturday morning came to an unfortunate end. Stu and Jack wheeled their creation out to the runway in the early morning, when the air was still cool. The small bright yellow craft was lined up with chocks on either side of the main wheels. Cries of "Brakes on", "Switches on" and "Contact" reminded me of my early flights in Tiger Moths.

After a couple of heaves on the propeller, the engine coughed once and sprang into roaring life. Jack leapt further back and stood ready to remove the chocks. Stu, in the cockpit, checked his few instruments as the engine warmed up. Eventually, Stu waved his hands in the time-honoured manner and Jack pulled away the nearest chocks before racing around the tail to do the same with the other set. A small round of applause sent the little plane on its way down the runway, slowly at first, then progressively increasing to about fifty knots. The tail came up and we watchers wondered whether Stu was going to be unwise enough to attempt to take off. We need not have worried. Something was going wrong with the aircraft now far distant along the runway. The two undercarriage struts moved symmetrically and gracefully outward, gently dumping the aircraft on its belly. The first bits to fly off were the shattered remains of the propeller, followed by the pitot tube, and portions of the wings. A Land Rover towing a long flatbed trailer went racing off to the sight of the disaster, where three or four young men tumbled out and began to extricate a fortunately undamaged Stuart before gathering the remains of the project on to the flatbed trailer.

The next attempt to get airborne came from 'Major Laugh'. About two weeks later his aircraft, unfinished in that it had not been painted, was lined up for an early Saturday morning test run. To everybody's surprise it completed three impressive tail-up runs along the runway without incident. Buoyed up by this success, and ignoring advice to the contrary, the Major decided there and then to carry out his first test flight. Several of those gathered around wondered aloud whether the intrepid new pilot, now resplendent in leather flying helmet and jacket, had ever flown anything before.

The question remained unanswered as the tiny aircraft roared once more down the runway and this time climbed unsteadily into the sky. It had been airborne for about thirty seconds and reached a height of perhaps sixty feet when it all ended. From a distance it looked as if the aircraft had stalled, then partially recovered, then descended under power to a cross between a heavy landing and a crash on the rough grass beyond the far end of the runway.

This time the pilot was not quite so lucky. He was conscious but seemed to have several broken ribs and some facial injuries as well as what might have been a broken leg. (It turned out not to be.) Remarkably he was still joking and smiling as his friends carried him away towards the sick bay.

As they loaded him gently into the back of the Land Rover I distinctly heard him say, "I suppose I should have taken a lesson and not just relied on the book."

****

The midsummer temperature was topping one hundred and ten in the shade, and the hot wind had started to blow out of the 'dead centre' which slowed things down even more. The very high temperatures and the skin-shrivelling hot dry wind made everything, even the simplest task, more difficult. Work out in the sun without skin protection for any length of time could result in hospitalisation. Inside the big metal hangars the environment was comparable with a sauna. The fire risk, in every activity around the base as well as in the surrounding forests had increased dramatically. An unwary driver clasping the door handle of a car that had been left out in the wind and in the sun could result in a severe burn. Some car owners, including ourselves, had taken the precaution of having the roof of the car painted white in an attempt to reflect the heat. This did have some effect but the conditions were so severe in early 1973 that even in these cars, plastic items could melt.

Most of the aircrew still loafed around drinking coffee and, where it was allowed, smoking. I had other things on my mind. I had received my marching orders. I was to return from Australia in mid-February, report to the Naval Air Station at Culdrose in Cornwall and undergo a conversion course to learn to fly the Sea King helicopter. After that I was to return to my old haunt at Portland as Senior Pilot of the Navy's Anti-Submarine Operational Flying Training Squadron, flying both the Sea King and the Wessex Mk 3.

More important than all this, was that my wife was now pregnant with the baby due in the late summer. She was having a very difficult time in the heat but nevertheless took on the mammoth task of preparing all our goods and chattels – which seemed to have multiplied alarmingly – for packing and shipping. I had to sell our two cars, which turned out to be surprisingly easy, particularly with the old Holden station wagon which doubled as Spoofy's kennel. In fact this represented probably the best motoring deal I have ever enjoyed, before or since. I had bought the car two years before for fifty dollars, did nothing to it except put petrol and a bit of oil into it, and finally sold it for fifty dollars.

One other task which proved difficult at first was the need to find a temporary home for Spoofy, our faithful companion over the last two years. His owners, Gordon and Sip Edgecombe, were coming to the end of their two-year secondment in England but there would be a three or four week gap between our departure and their arrival back in Nowra. Sip had made arrangements for a local couple to look after the dog during the gap weeks. In fact it turned out to be the same couple who had agreed originally to take Spoofy in for the whole two-year absence of his owners. On that occasion they had backed out at the last minute, and having agreed to help once more, they changed their minds again and let everybody down for the second time. This unwelcome news spurred Irene into action and within a few days she had resolved the problem. Spoofy would not be homeless.

The last few days passed all too quickly. I filled in forms and agreed all the travel arrangements with the Navy Movements people. The international removal team turned up and packed every item of our belongings as though each piece of doubtful crockery was a precious heirloom. Spoofy sat gloomily watching this day long activity but brightened considerably when the team left and he saw that we – especially his toddler playmate – were still in residence. The next day he was taken to his new temporary home and we said goodbye to him for the last time. Everyone except the dog was saddened by this. He had taken the metaphorical deep breath and moved on once more.

Once everything had gone and we were left with only the bare necessities we found ourselves leaning on the generosity of two British friends, Chris and Sue Olsen, who lived just around the corner. Chris had started out as a Buccaneer pilot in the Royal Navy but following the Wilson Government's perverse decision to do away with the British aircraft carriers, Chris had transferred to Australia where he flew the Skyhawk. A few years after we left he moved on again to become a successful airline pilot.

Eventually we bade goodbye to our friends and climbed aboard a local taxi which took us the short distance to Nowra's railway station. The late summer sky was a dome of brilliant clear blue and despite the early morning, the temperature was already climbing above ninety. The air was still fairly dry in Nowra and a light breeze took the edge off the heat. We knew that these relatively benign conditions couldn't last and we were not proved wrong.

We each took our last view in silence of the little country town which had been our home for longer than any other. For our daughter it had been the only home she had known. It was a sad and thoughtful little group that occupied the bouncing clanking carriage as it rolled north towards Sydney. We thought of friends and colleagues, of neighbours, of the vicar, the postman, the shopkeepers and most of all, of a big-hearted, loving, irrepressible black dog. We were gone and in all probability we would never see any of them again.

By the time the train reached Sydney the temperature had risen well past a hundred degrees and the humidity was trying to catch up. We alighted to a hot noisy sweaty throng, gathered our nine large cases and pushchair together and looked around for a taxi big enough to accommodate us all. The journey to the airport was mercifully short as every inch of the big station wagon was packed with luggage leaving uncomfortably little room for passengers. The taxi was air-conditioned which the driver helpfully augmented by opening his side window in order to rest his elbow on the ledge.

Our homeward journey across Australia was a test of patience and fortitude. By the time we had loaded ourselves into an aircraft provided by 'Reg Ansett's Airlines of Australia' at Sydney the humidity had hit jackpot and the rain was pouring in solid curtains, hammering vertically into the tarmac as only tropical rain seems able to do. We waited beyond the take-off time as the pilots made conflicting announcements of how they were going to get to Perth and I imagined them tossing a coin to decide between a fuel stop at Adelaide or Melbourne. I was not impressed. In the event, we went to Melbourne where most of the passengers' baggage was off-loaded and left behind on the tarmac in the rain. The ride was one of the most turbulent and rough journeys I have ever taken by air. Passengers were airsick and we experienced a remarkable in-flight tableau when the beautiful blonde air hostess, called by an airsick girl and temporarily distracted from her attempt to chat up a handsome young man, responded to the distressed passenger with a memorable "Aw shaddup!"

When eventually we arrived in Perth several hours late, in the middle of the night and bereft of our luggage, our previously booked hotel – booked through the airline – seemed to have forgotten our existence.

Things got better, we enjoyed our time in the sophisticated city of Perth, and then for a further two weeks in Singapore, following a flight from Perth wrapped and cosseted in the comfort and style of Quantas, before we made our weary way once more to yet another airport to board the RAF trooping flight to Brize Norton in a VC10 of Transport Command.

To my surprise I discovered that I had been nominated as the Officer in Charge of the passengers. This grand sounding title was actually fairly meaningless and I discovered that in reality my new status ranked some way below the leading aircraftsman cabin attendant. My one moment to exercise power came towards the end of the refuelling stop at Colombo, where Rebecca was an instant hit with a group of saffron-robed monks who seemed to be able to communicate fluently with her despite the absence of a mutual language. As we were re-boarding the aircraft after sitting around in the sun for half an hour or so, I climbed the boarding ladder to find my way barred by the prissy leading aircraftsman cabin attendant. "Boarding pass, sir," he announced with a smirk. I hadn't noticed the same question being put to my fellow passengers but I let that pass.

"It's in my jacket pocket." I indicated the jacket of my Gieves lightweight suit which was draped across my seat. The boarding pass could be seen quite clearly, sticking out of the inside pocket of the folded jacket.

"You need to have it with you." The crowd was building up on the steps behind me

"Well, it is there, in my jacket, as you can see." I was becoming terse.

The man persisted in his 'jobsworth' pose. "I can't let you on board without a boarding pass," he mouthed stubbornly as he continued to block the door.

I was by now a very unhappy bunny and my fellow passengers were becoming equally unhappy as they stood and cooked in the hot tropical sun on the boarding steps behind me. I leaned conspiratorially towards my antagonist. "You have three choices," I said quietly through gritted teeth as I glared at the lanky twerp. "One, you go and fetch the bloody Captain. Two, I go back to the terminal and as I am supposed to be in charge of the passengers I can't leave without me, or Three, I throw you down these steps and we leave without you." He caught the look in my eye and stood aside. Throughout the rest of the flight he tried hard to be difficult as he simpered up and down the narrow aisle between the backward facing seats but I left communication with him to Irene. Sweet reasonableness coupled with a steely determination to stand no nonsense soon brought him to heel.

Eventually we touched down on the main runway at RAF Brize Norton in Oxfordshire. It was two o'clock in the morning but most of the body clocks were working on eleven a.m. Some were wide awake, others who had been unable to sleep were walking automatons. Everybody was weary from the long flight and wanted to get away from the airport to home and rest.

As we trailed off the aircraft we were shuffled into RAF buses by the terse and officious Movements staff and then driven the short distance to a large empty hangar where a line of trestle tables had been set up. Behind the tables waited a row of unsmiling customs officers. The air was bitterly cold and the wind had been blowing a light drizzle into our faces.

Our luggage had been retrieved from the aircraft hold and passengers were trying to identify their cases. Several piles of cases were quite big and ours was bigger than most. I had no idea how we were going to move it. We joined a queue filing past the trestle tables as one by one the weary travellers were engaged by customs officers. I found myself facing a pimply youth in the slightly scruffy uniform of a customs officer, sporting a single gold stripe on each sleeve. "Anything to declare?" he asked woodenly. I heard Rebecca, who had been sleeping, start to cry.

"No," I replied. "All we have are personal effects already imported into Australia."

"What about that watch?" He pointed at my Seiko and held out his hand. I slipped the watch from my wrist and held it out to him. He took it without a word and started to examine it minutely, before placing it on the table between us. "And that one," he grunted, as he pointed towards Irene who was holding Rebecca in her arms. I took the child. She handed over the watch and it was examined as before, then placed beside my watch on the table. I was aware that we were getting special treatment as other passengers were passing us by and heading for the far side of the hangar where more buses were waiting to take them either to the 'terminal' or to the rather austere Transit Hotel where they would wait for onward transport.

The young customs officer pointed rudely at my wife and demanded her handbag. He rummaged through it and placed it to one side then his eyes lit on the cameras we were each carrying. Irene had a thirty-five millimetre camera. I had another still camera but I also had a bag over my shoulder housing a cine camera purchased in Kiama during our first year. These were placed in front of what I now regarded as an irritating young upstart and they each received a cursory examination. Eventually he looked up and shoved the watches and still cameras across the table. "OK. You can go," he said in the manner of the desk sergeant letting last night's drunk out of the cells. Irene retrieved her handbag and I scooped up two cameras and our watches before turning and walking away. I had gone only four or five paces before I realised that I no longer had the cine camera. At that point all the frustrations, irritation, pettiness and tiredness boiled over. Leaving Irene with Rebecca, I charged up to the young official, rudely stepped in front of his next customer and demanded loudly, "Where's my camera?"

"You've got them," he said.

"I put a total of three cameras on your table while you wasted my time and you gave me back two. Where's the other one?" I snarled, ready now to lean across the narrow board separating us and grab him by his scrawny acne-covered neck. One of the other customs officers, an older man, looked up from what he was writing and moved towards us. "What's the problem?" he asked as he approached.

Beside myself by now with travel weariness, frustration and fury, I bellowed, "That bastard has stolen my cine camera." All heads within five yards turned in my direction. The two customs men looked at each other then the younger one's complexion turned a sickly shade of scarlet. He opened his mouth and spluttered something incomprehensible. His older colleague fished under the table where there must have been some sort of shelf. His hand emerged holding my camera case. Wordlessly he handed the camera across the table to me.

"A misunderstanding," he muttered, then he added, "None of your stuff is dutiable anyway". He glanced at his now silent and deflated companion. The cockiness and arrogance had gone. He was just a gangly kid in a second-hand uniform. I snatched the camera back, throwing at both of them "He stole my camera. Don't say he didn't. He took it and put it behind his desk." I took them both in with a look of disgust, turned on my heel and stalked off. I didn't get a round of applause but the excited buzz suggested a note of approval. My lasting impression of the obnoxious youth in the blue uniform was of a face and neck covered in livid pimples, some the size, or so it seemed, of miniature volcanoes.

'Welcome back to England!' I thought as we all set off for the other side of the vast hangar to where a group of 'meeters and greeters' was gathered. My father and mother were standing there looking frozen in the pre-dawn light. They swept us up and away. Our antipodean adventure was over.

Chapter 22

Aftermath

I had been back in England about three months when I first heard rumour of the disaster that had befallen the Australian Fleet Air Arm. I had settled the family in a charming little holiday cottage down by the Helford River while I set about learning the rudiments of flying the Sea King. In midwinter there was almost no demand for the holiday homes scattered around West Cornwall, so we wallowed in gentle isolation while I completed the Sea King course and then planned the move into married quarters in Weymouth, ready to take up my new role at Portland.

I was uncomfortable with my time at Culdrose, the huge naval helicopter base near Helston. I was particularly uncomfortable with the treatment, control and direction of the officers under training at various levels but my usual response to difficulties with the Service hierarchy had been to keep a low profile, get my head down and concentrate on the job in hand. This worked fairly well until shortly before I was due to 'graduate' and leave for Portland. Suddenly, the word was out that an 'Escape and Evasion' exercise was to take place. These exercises took place every three years or so and were designed to train and test aircrew in the techniques of avoiding capture by an enemy force and then, having been captured, to enjoy the experience of dealing with likely enemy interrogation techniques. They normally lasted three or four days, when hundreds of aircrew would be dumped in flying kit, and not much else, in a remote region such as Dartmoor. Troops, largely paratroops or Royal Marines would then comprise the search and capture force. The fleeing aircrew would be given routes to follow to 'escape' but the whole thing was designed so that most would live rough for a few days and then undergo an interrogation. The living rough element was not considered much of a problem but the interrogation phase could be uncomfortable with horrible stories in circulation of the effects of sensory deprivation, white noise, intense cold and some physical roughness. However, provided a sense of proportion was maintained not many individuals viewed the thing as much more than a necessary irritation.

On this occasion, some genius at headquarters, or possibly somewhere in between, had invented a form for all the 'escapees' to sign before the exercise began, in which the Navy, the Government and anyone else involved would be absolved of any responsibility for any injury, or even death, that might befall the participants. People were generally very unhappy with this development and few appreciated the need for the Navy to demand signatures on such a 'blood chit' bearing in mind the normal rules which apply within the armed services. What were our armchair masters planning to do to us?

I decided I would have no truck with this nasty piece of bureaucratic nonsense and I politely refused to sign the document. I was apparently one of only about six or seven among the many hundreds of officers at Culdrose who refused to sign the form. Nobody took this course lightly because we all realised that to react in the way we had, in a disciplined service, even when in the right, was likely to produce a bad reaction among the local brass. It did. A few days before I was due to complete my conversion course and leave, I was sent for by Commander Air. I went across to the control tower, climbed the steps to the important persons offices and joined two other officers, both of whom I knew, waiting in the outer office.

We were ushered into the 'presence' and assembled in a row, standing in front of a large wooden desk behind which sat a tiny man dressed in neat flying overalls. We three stood like naughty schoolboys sent before the headmaster. There were no words of introduction. No greeting. The little man just glared at us. I had encountered him some years previously and although I conceded that he might have been kind to children and animals my own opinion, formed then and unchanged now, was that he was a nasty, poisonous little man. Brash, pompous, aloof and vain, I thought. I tried with some success to hide my irritation and contempt, but kept my voice polite and even, as I responded to his aggressive and rude questioning. I attempted to explain that I had absolutely no objection to going on the Escape and Evasion exercise but I saw no reason to sign away any right to redress in the case of injury. I was serving under the terms of the Naval Discipline Act, and no such waiver forms were necessary. I would go but I wouldn't sign, I repeated at length. My two companions adopted much the same response, all to no avail. The horrible little despot continued to snarl up at us in his travesty of an interview. His parting shot was that this misbehaviour would go on our records.

"Misbehaviour? What misbehaviour?" responded one of my companions. "And what do you mean?" then, after a long pause, "sir."

I found out a few days later when I took my leave of the Station. I passed the course but the brief report contained a single mean-minded remark. I could guess the author.

Later, when I joined my new squadron at Portland I discovered that the batch of 'blood chits' sent to that Station had gone straight into the nearest bin.

In the event the exercise was a disaster, or certainly it was for the planners and organisers. On the start day, teams of Safety Equipment and Survival Instructors boosted by headquarters staff officers descended on all the operational naval airfields located in England and, erroneously assuming they still had the element of surprise, they bundled aircrew into trucks and buses to be whisked off to various drop-off points around Dartmoor. There they were met with more directing staff who briefed them in small groups as to what they were supposed to do and where their first check points were.

The search force, consisting of several hundred troops from the Royal Marines boosted by interrogators from the Intelligence Corps were to deploy the next day – to give them a head start, the fugitive aviators were told.

One curious aspect that surprised the directing staff somewhat was that nobody seemed apprehensive as to what was to come, nor did anyone appear to be irritated by their routines and plans being so rudely and precipitately disrupted. The exercise planners and organisers were of course completely unaware that the metaphorical cat had been out of the bag ever since the daft 'blood chit' exercise had been launched. The laid-back, smiling aviators knew when the exercise had been due to start, and where it would take place. Most of them had made plans.

Cars, bicycles and motorbikes had been secreted at various points all over the moor. Wives and girlfriends had been issued with pick-up instructions for later that night. Food caches, with maps, torches, money, clothing and even Citizens' Band radios had been hidden.

By the time the briefings were complete it was late morning and a thin mist, impregnated with drizzle, had descended on the moor. Bands of half a dozen or so green-clad happy wanderers were released and began to disappear into the mist. The instructors were perplexed. Most of the departing aircrew were chatting and joking and some were even whistling happily as they strode away.

Once clear of the instructors the small groups ignored the directions they had been given and headed for the paths and tracks that criss-cross the moor. By nightfall or shortly afterwards most of the supply caches had been located and put to use. One or two of the vehicles laden with what looked like farm labourers were already heading away from the moor as fast as they could and other vehicles were driving slowly along some of the bigger roads, headlights ablaze, making beacons for the wandering aircrew. By the first few hours after midnight an estimated three quarters of the men who had been dumped around the moor that morning were already well clear of the exercise area. Of the others, some regarded as super keen, were intent on playing the game and pressing on with the exercise and others, some of whom were thought to be a bit dim, were lost, having failed to locate either vehicles or supply dumps. Nearly two hundred young men had been launched into the exercise. By dawn the next morning less than forty were still on the moor and half a dozen of these escaped that morning. The search force combed the moor with skill and efficiency but by the end of the day they had only about twelve prisoners – mostly those who had become lost. Of the remainder, the very fact that there were so few of them crossing a vast space enabled most of them to keep out of the hands of the searchers and in some noteworthy cases, occasionally skirting round rendezvous points where traps had been set, they not only made it across the moor to the finish line but continued on, in character, to re-enter their air stations clandestinely.

The third day of the five earmarked for the exercise seemed to be progressing well and it was said that the Admiral and his senior staff were preening themselves on the skill exhibited by 'their lads' in outwitting the 'bootnecks'. The lieutenant colonel commanding the Royal Marine Commandos was not at all happy. A suspicious man at the best of times he smelled a rat. Deeply suspicious of the failure of his troops to root out their quarry, and noting the rapidly clearing weather, he decided to cheat. He requisitioned a Gazelle reconnaissance helicopter from the Third Brigade Air Squadron and had himself flown around the moor.

All he could see were dispersed groups comprised of three or four commandos methodically scouring the moor. There was not a single aircrew fugitive to be seen anywhere. This confirmed his suspicion that in his mind 'a gigantic fraud' had been perpetrated on his men. The honour of the unit was at stake. He ordered the pilot to return him to the Naval Air Command Headquarters at the Royal Naval Air Station, Yeovilton, as quickly as possible – although he put the instruction in rather more earthy terms. While using the UHF radio he demanded an interview with the Admiral that afternoon.

Before the colonel was even halfway back to Yeovilton, an even bigger bombshell landed – in the afternoon post. Overcome with the success of their escape pranks, several silly young men who were at that time enjoying the comforts of different hotels in Torquay decided to rub in their triumph over the Admiral and his staff. The afternoon post delivered a bundle of saucy seaside postcards addressed to the Admiral, his Chief of Staff and others. 'Wish you were here', repeated several times, was the most polite of the messages written on the backs of the anonymous cards.

The mood at Headquarters turned from elation to grim anger. The Admiral broke a pencil. The Duty Staff Officer was instructed to organise raids on every hotel in and around Torquay. The Staff Legal Advisor tried in vain to explain that the Navy could not raid commercial or private premises without the authority of the police – unless they were looking to arrest deserters.

"Right, call all the bastards deserters then!" shrieked the Admiral. Nobody was bold enough to challenge that and a couple of small bands from the Devonport Provost Marshal's office set off in pursuit of two hundred officer deserters. The reporter on the *Plymouth Argus* could not believe what he was hearing when this latest piece of tasty information was relayed to him by his mole in the Devonport base telephone exchange.

Later that afternoon, two incidents occurred, both concerning courting couples. In a shady lay-by just outside Torquay, a car door was wrenched open by a sailor wearing a white belt and gaiters over his uniform while his companion, another Leading Patrolman, compared a photograph held in his hand to the appearance of the unfortunate young man being hauled out of the car with his shirt tail flapping around him. The young lady in the car began to scream as she pushed her thin cotton dress back down towards her knees and tried unsuccessfully to retrieve a small pair of scarlet silk knickers drawn out of the car onto the road in the scuffle and now drifting away on the light breeze. Up on the moor, to the east of Princetown a similar incident was taking place, with the exception that the arresting team consisted of hefty Royal Marines one of whom had sustained a deep bite in his forearm following an unfortunate encounter with an unrestrained breast of significant proportions. The pain in his arm and the attack on the nearby corporal caused them to treat the young man, who by now was naked below the waist, with more than the minimum force necessary to restrain him. Blood was pouring from the nose of the junior barrister as he tried to raise his head out of the muddy puddle it was pressed into. The sergeant poked his head inadvisably into the car in an attempt to calm the half dressed screaming banshee inside and explain the situation when he was struck forcibly above his left eye and below his cap badge with a four inch stiletto heel. As he staggered backwards he heard the Marine kneeling on his captive in the road saying, "'Ere Sarge, I think we got the wrong one."

Within the hour the whole exercise was called off. It was said that the Admiral had been summoned to Whitehall to explain himself to the First Sea Lord. The poor man was never the same until he retired a few months later.

****

While all this was going on I was trying to pin down the rumours of what had happened shortly after my departure from Australia. Eventually, I succeeded. It seemed the Australian Navy had been placed suddenly in the market for a few new aircraft.

The two Tracker Squadrons were both billeted in the same large hangar at Nowra, when the front line squadron was ashore. Whereas the administrative offices, briefing rooms, stores and so forth of the helicopter squadrons were situated in huts some distance from the dispersal area and the big hangar bordering it, this was not the case with the Trackers. Their huge hangar was arranged with rows of rooms set along the insides of the three sides which did not open. Thus the squadron offices, briefing facilities and ready rooms, as well as all the toolboxes, records, machinery, tractors, and maintenance kit – in fact every single thing that went to make up a squadron – was stored within the hangar.

A young maintenance rating – a sailor – as the Aussies designated him, had been arraigned before the Captain charged with sleeping on watch and being absent from his place of duty. He had protested his innocence but had nevertheless been found guilty and sentenced to twenty-one days' stoppage of leave with extra work and drill. Some believed this to be a fairly harsh punishment but the Navy way was to accept a possible injustice, take your punishment and get on with your life. This man however harboured a serious grudge. He was going to miss out on a long weekend holiday, he was probably going to lose his girlfriend of three weeks and he reckoned that his defending officer had done a pretty lousy job. In this latter assertion a lot of his compatriots as well as some officers apparently thought he was right.

Three days after he had begun his punishment, on the Friday at the beginning of a holiday weekend, he was detailed off as the Squadron Duty Rating, responsible for securing the squadron when everyone else went off on leave, locking up the hangar and returning the keys to the guardroom.

The man started his duties in his usual diligent manner, going around inside the hangar checking that the individual office doors were locked and the lights switched off. He checked that all the aircraft were in a safe configuration with wheels chocked and nothing leaking. He wound shut the last section of the big front door and then started sorting out the keys for the external locks. At about this point, his sense of burning resentment boiled over. He felt hard done by, isolated and, in his terms "Deeply pissed off". He had intended to take a 'wet' in the canteen after returning the keys before walking across to his mess in one of the accommodation blocks when he realised he didn't have his wallet. At first he thought he had left it in his locker in his mess but then a niggling worm of worry started to creep around inside his head. What if he had lost it? There wasn't much money at stake but the wallet contained his driving licence and, most important, his Naval ID card. To be found without his identity card would be a punishable offence and he would be in the shit again – as if he wasn't in enough already!

At that point he seemed to have decided he had had enough. He went back into the hangar, switching on lights as he went. He headed straight for the neat rows of aircraft, stopping at each one to unscrew the fuel drain and the gravity filler. Allowing the high octane avgas – petrol, that is – to spill out over the clean white concrete floor of the hangar.

Because of the danger from volatile fuel vapour it is the usual policy to fill the fuel tanks of aircraft before they are stowed away in a hangar. If there is no airspace in the tank there is minimal risk of a potentially explosive mixture of air and fuel vapour forming.

When all the fuel cocks were open several thousand gallons of high octane petrol was swilling around the floor of the hangar. The disaffected duty sailor then stepped out through the small personnel door set into the main door, paused to light an illegal cigarette before throwing the still lit match in through the door. The force of the initial explosion was directed largely upward, demolishing the hangar roof which collapsed in on the furiously burning aircraft below.

The arsonist was himself blown several feet backward by the force of the explosion but was uninjured apart from being heavily singed. As he ran from the heat of the flames and the subsequent explosion he tripped and fell becoming mildly concussed.

In the subsequent enquiry, the sailor declared that it had been his intention to hurl his unhappy self into the inferno he had created "but it was too hot" he said. Nobody believed him.

Despite this being the most prominent account pieced together from several sources, after a while a new theory began to take shape. According to this new rumour, the Australian Navy, or perhaps the government, had reached the conclusion that their force of twelve Grumman S2F Tracker aircraft were showing their age and were rapidly approaching obsolescence. They needed to be replaced but they couldn't afford to buy upgraded replacements from the United States.

In the event this potential disaster turned out to have an upside. The United States Government quickly became alarmed at what they considered to be a major loss of anti-submarine capability in the Far East and so they offered to replace the fleet of fixed-wing anti-submarine aircraft with another dozen aircraft, being almost the latest version of the Tracker. The offer was quickly accepted and all became well again.

Which version was the correct one? Nobody knows.

Crafty Aussies!